Gay Theatre Alliance Directory of Gay Plays

Gay Theatre Alliance Directory of Gay Plays

Compiled and edited and
with an introduction by
Terry Helbing

JH Press
New York, New York

Copyright © 1980 JH Press

All rights reserved. No part of this book may be reproduced in any form or by any means without the prior written permission of the Publisher, excepting brief quotes used in connection with reviews written specifically for inclusion in a magazine or newspaper.

First printing, January 1980.

Printed in the United States of America.

Library of Congress Cataloging in Publication Data

Helbing, Terry, 1951-
   Gay Theatre Alliance directory of gay plays.

    Includes index.
    1. Homosexuality — Drama — Directories. 2. American drama — Directories. 3. English drama — Directories. I. Gay Theatre Alliance. II. Title. III. Title: Directory of gay plays.
PS338.H66H4   016.812'008'0353   79-91529
ISBN 0-935672-00-1
1   2   3   4   5   —   84   83   82   81   80

For my father

TABLE OF CONTENTS

	Page
Introduction	1
Key To Listings	7
Alphabetical Listings of Plays	9
Appendix A: "Lost" Plays	115
Appendix B: Gay Theatre Companies	117
Index of Playwrights	119
Listing Forms for Gay Plays	123
Gay Theatre Alliance Membership Information	129

Acknowledgments

Thank you to Jim O'Quinn for his legwork; to Loretta Lotman, Owen Wilson, William M. Hoffman and Douglas Stewart for their bibliographies; to Robert Chesley, Charles Gilman and especially Lee Barton for their assistance in finding the unusual and obscure plays; and to Deborah Rose, Allan Estes and particularly Doric Wilson for their continued support.

Introduction

Here, for the first time in book form, is comprehensive information on plays with major gay characters and/or predominant gay themes. The emphasis is on *major* and *predominant,* since plays with one minor gay character or that only touch upon gayness peripherally have not been included in this book. Those plays which might be described as being of the "Grand Hotel" genre — set in some public place (a bar, an all-night diner, etc.) and having large casts that usually include a black, a prostitute, an alcoholic, a junkie,and a gay man and/or lesbian — have been eliminated. Instead, the plays included in this directory have gayness or gay people (male and female) as their main, primary, or at least, very important focus, theme or concern.

Naturally, anytime you try to set up such definite criteria, you run into problems with borderline cases. Some may disagree with the decisions made as to which side of the dividing line some of these plays have been placed. One of the most difficult plays in this regard that can serve as a general example is Lanford Wilson's *The 5th of July,* which is at the same time the ultimate gay play and not a gay play at all. In it, two of the major characters are gay men who are lovers. But like so many of Wilson's plays, all of the eight characters in the play are major characters, and the gayness of the two men is given the same treatment accorded the other characters' age, height, hair color or profession. That is, their gayness is not an issue, a problem or a subject of the play — it is simply taken for granted. Many, if not most, gay theatre people might see this as the goal of examining the gay experience onstage: to have gayness comfortably accepted or assimilated into the human experience. Without arguing the good or bad points of such a goal, we are obviously nowhere near such general acceptance of gay characters and gay theatre at the end of the 1970's — therefore, the play was not included. As this directory indicates, an ever-increasing number of gay men and lesbians find it useful and necessary to explore the rich variety of the gay experience more directly in theatrical forms. (Of course, not all gay plays are written by gay playwrights. Many writers believe that to be accomplished at their art, they must be able to write sensitively about the entire spectrum of human experience. Therefore, inclusion of the work of any author in this directory does not necessarily mean that the author is gay.)

Also not included here are plays in which homosexuality is an important factor, but is not handled directly in the onstage action. This would include many plays written prior to 1970, including some by Tennessee Williams. Brick's possible homosexuality in *Cat On A Hot Tin Roof* and Sebastian Venable's attraction to young boys in *Suddenly Last Summer* are undeniably important elements of these plays, but the homosexuality involved offstage triggers the on-stage events and does not take center stage. Even more important, information about Tennessee Williams' plays and others of this kind is readily available from existing reference works.

Finally, not included here are many examples of that particular gay entertainment genre variously called "drag/transvestite/radical camp" theatre. While much of the work of such people as the Theatre of the Ridiculous (Ronald Tavel), the Ridiculous Theatrical Company (Charles Ludlam), Hot Peaches, the Angels of Light and others definitely reflects the marvelously free spirit of the gay sensibility, many such groups refuse to be pinned down by the term "gay theatre," feeling that it is too limiting a description of their work.

What remains, then, are detailed descriptions, and where applicable, production and publication history, of some 400 plays that deal directly with the lives and concerns of gay men and women. As work on finding these plays progressed, the task became more and more like a detective hunt, since so often gay plays appeared, played a few days or weeks — often at out-of-the-way locations — closed, and were never heard from again. In some cases, playwrights could be found in the Manhattan telephone directory. Other playwrights could not be located so easily, but eventually a friend of a friend of a

DIRECTORY OF GAY PLAYS 3

business associate of a director or a scene designer knew the last address the playwright had two years ago, and the author was finally located. Some listings were obtained from actors who appeared in the plays and saved their scripts; others came from conscientious theatregoers who saved their gay-play programs, "knowing they would be valuable someday." (Several people who were very helpful in this search are mentioned in the Acknowledgments.)

Especially interesting in this regard are early gay plays like Edouard Bourdet's **The Captive,** Mae West's **The Drag,** Mordaunt Shairp's **The Green Bay Tree** and Wolcott Gibb's **Season in the Sun.** These plays have been discussed elsewhere; however, two newly unearthed plays of historical interest merit special attention. **At Saint Judas's** by Henry B. Fuller is a one-act curiosity about a bridegroom who discovers that his best man is deeply in love with him ten minutes before he is to be married. It is the only play with gay content in a twelve-play collection by Fuller that was published in New York in 1896. It is not known if the play was ever performed. **Game of Fools** by James (Barr) Fugate was written in the 1950's and published in a limited, numbered and signed edition of 2,000 copies by One, Inc., one of the few homophile organizations active during that period. Fugate had no formal education or dramatic training. He admitted in his Introduction that he was not a professional writer, but rather "an amateur propagandist" who "earned his living as an oil field roustabout" and lived in Kansas "in proletarian simplicity." While his story of trumped up arrest and imprisonment may seem unrealistic and melodramatic now, no doubt at the time it was an impassioned plea for tolerance and understanding. Once again, it is not known if the play was ever produced. Both of these plays were located by Charles Gilman, owner of the WaltWhitman Bookshop in San Francisco, who specializes in rare and out-of-print gay books.

While there is still a scarcity of lesbian material, some new plays were discovered in the compiling of this directory, most notably Jill Posener's **Any Woman Can**, Micheline Wandor's **Care and Control**, Jane Staab's **December to May**, Susie Chancey's **First Lover**, collectively performed by the Cambridge Lesbian Theatre; **An Oral Herstory of Lesbianism,** collectively created by thirteen women from an idea by Terry Wolverton; Kate Kasten's **On the Elevator**, Carol Pugliese's **The Other Side of Silence**, **Play** by Shelly Zaikis, and others.

The listings are not limited to the United States. Numerous plays by English, Canadian and Irish playwrights are represented, as well as the collectively created work of the men and women of London's Gay Sweatshop. Of particular interest here are two plays: **The Leather Man** by West German Hans Eppendorfer, and **Rents** by Michael Wilcox, which details gay life in Edinburgh, Scotland and was one of the successes of the Edinburgh International Theatre Festival this past summer. Hopefully, future editions of this book will include more international gay plays.

As the final manuscript for the book was being prepared, a number of common concerns became apparent among a disparate group of playwrights scattered across the country and the world. Overwhelmingly, the central theme — and the most often used word in this book — is *relationship*. In all of its permutations and combinations, writers of gay plays have the gay relationship on their minds. Of course this reflects our whole society's concern for the way people do and do not interact with one another in the late 1970's, but some of the preoccupation with relationships is of special concern to the gay culture.

Some of the earlier plays listed suffer from what a friend once called "heterosexist perversive mimicry," a wonderful and strange combination of words describing gay people's inclination to imitate straight monogamous relationships since they had no role models of their own. These plays present a gay couple aping conventional married life, and in some cases, fantasizing about gay male pregnancy. By the later 1970's though, most of the "relationship plays" try to find their way through and understand the new territory that gays are exploring in their romantic interactions. While there is still some evidence of romanticism in the search for "the man of my dreams," many more of the plays (particularly the male ones) are examining the ways gay men find to deal with each other, forging ahead without any role models to follow. These dealings also reflect the contemporary urban lifestyle of many gay men in that a great number of plays describe "two gay men who share an apartment" and who are/are not lovers, and how the two men in question respond to outside influences on their relationship. Note the number of **Male First Name and Male First Name** plays listed here as evidence of this trend!

A subdivision of the "relationship plays" is the "old/young" plays, which describe the difficulties encountered in relationships between men who are separated by a number of years. Since many object to the emphasis placed on youth and beauty in the gay male subculture, it is logical that this subject matter would appear often in gay plays.

Coming out is also an important part of many gay plays: even though it has been over ten years since the Stonewall Riots which began the latest phase of the gay liberation movement, the conservative trend of recent years has made it difficult for another generation of gay people to acknowledge their homosexuality openly. Coming out remains a traumatic, but finally liberating, experience which is often dealt with theatrically. A subcategory of the "coming out" plays might be labeled "the old college friend" plays: s/he is often the cause for the first stirrings of homosexual feelings in many characters in these plays, but all too often, those feelings never have a chance to be fully expressed and appreciated and occur furtively, if at all.

While the lesbian plays listed share these concerns to varying degrees, gay women are more often interested in history, or rather, "herstory": images of important women of the past who are of invaluable assistance to contemporary gay women in finding their positive gay identity.

• • •

The listings of the plays are presented alphabetically by title and contain information on the author, type of play (drama, comedy, etc.), number of acts, number of male and/or female characters, number of interior and exterior settings, plot synopsis, location and date of first production (if produced), book title, publisher, and date of publication (if published), amateur royalties, the name and address of the playwright's agent, if applicable, and if a musical, if and in what form the score is available. The information is presented in a standard format for consistency and ease of reading. A key to the listing format is presented before the first page of alphabetical listings. Dollar amounts, when quoted, are for amateur performances only. It is assumed that royalties for semi-professional and professional productions will be negotiated in accordance with minimums set forth by the Dramatists Guild, or other such contracts equitable to the playwright. Since amateur rights for many of the plays are controlled by the two major amateur leasing companies, Dramatists Play Service and Samuel French (New York and London), their addresses are not repeated each time they occur, but are listed on the Key to Listings page instead. The alphabetical listings of playwrights' names in the Index will be of assistance in finding the work of particular authors.

Producers, theatre companies or individuals interested in reading any of the scripts listed in this book should contact the agent indicated for the play, and mention that they saw the play listed in the *Gay Theatre Alliance Directory of Gay Plays*. When no agent is listed, they should contact the Northeast Regional Office of the Gay Theatre Alliance, 51 West 4th Street, Room 300, New York, N.Y. 10012, which is maintaining an up-to-date address file of all playwrights included here.

While this book may be a comprehensive listing of gay plays, it is admittedly, unfortunately, not complete. Appendix A contains a list of "lost" plays, for which complete information could not be located before the printing deadline. After the book is published, I'm sure many of these and other playwrights will come forward, asking "Why weren't my plays included?" I hope they do — I encourage them and their friends to contact the Gay Theatre Alliance with their whereabouts and information about their work. Samples of the listings form used to compile this directory are included at the back of the book, and may be used to send listings for plays not included. The *Gay Theatre Alliance Directory of Gay Plays* is not a finished product, but an ongoing project; revised editions that include plays not located for this edition and gay plays yet to be written will be published as needed.

The plays that are included in this first edition represent a large number and wide cross-section of plays and playwrights concerned with portraying the gay experience. Together, they demonstrate to theatre people and to gay men and women that there is a lot more going on in gay theatre than **Norman, Is That You?** and **Boys In the Band**.

— *Terry Helbing*
December 1979

Key to Listings

Each play listed in this directory follows a standard format. The following listing describes the format in general terms (not all plays will have every item listed):

Title of Play by Author. Type of play. Number of acts. (If musical, form in which score is available.) Number of male characters, number of female characters (if more than one role can be played by the same actor, indicated by "Doubling"). Number of interior and/or exterior settings. Amateur royalties for first/succeeding performances. Prod: if produced, theatre or theatre company, location and date of first production. Publ: if published, book title (if different from play title), publisher, location and date of publication. Agent: if playwright has an agent, agent's name and address.

Plot synopsis or description of the events of the play.

A few other abbreviations are used:

Repr = settings for the play can be done representationally.
Comp = composite set; a number of settings included on the stage at the same time; also called "unit set."
Negotiable = author or agent will negotiate with producer on royalties to be paid.
q.v. = a cross-reference to another play listing.

To avoid repetition, the addresses of the two major leasing agencies for amateur rights are listed here and not repeated every time they appear in the directory:

Dramatists Play Service, Inc.
440 Park Avenue South
New York, N.Y. 10016

Samuel French, Inc.
25 West 45th Street
New York, N.Y. 10036

Samuel French Ltd. (London)
26 Southampton Street
Strand WC2 England

A

Ad Hoc Committee, The by Doric Wilson. Comedy. One act. 12M, 2F. 1 interior. $40/$35. Agent: Terry Helbing, 51 West 4th Street, Room 300, New York, N.Y. 10012.

A political satire: the characters of **Street Theatre** (q.v.) two months after the Stonewall as they attempt to form a gay political organization.

Adeline by James Purdy. Drama. One act. 2M. 1 interior. Prod: Herbert Berghof Studio, New York, 1979. Agent: Gilbert Parker, Curtis Brown, Ltd., 575 Madison Avenue, New York, N.Y. 10022.

The love-hate relationship between two young men, set in a small town in the South. Though ostensibly about their quarrel over a girl, the play has homosexual overtones.

Age of Consent by Drew Griffiths and Kate Crutchley. Drama. Full length. 4M, 2F. 1 interior. Prod: Gay Sweatshop, London, 1977.

Collectively devised by the Gay Sweatshop, the play is a Theatre-in-Education-type show for the sixteen-year-old age group. The love affair of a twenty-year-old and a twenty-eight-year-old man is discovered by the police.

All the News That's Fit to Print by Steph Martin. Drama. One act. 1M, 2F. 1 interior.

Two lesbians give a party for their straight neighbor prior to one of the women's departure on a cross-country trip.

Along the Bent and Narrow by Owen Wilson. Drama-comedy. Two acts. 2M, 2F. 1 interior. Prod: Church of the Beloved Disciple, New York, 1975.

A play about people who accept part-time marginal relationships in their lives, set in Greenwich Village, New York.

Altar Boys by Stephen Magowan. Drama. Two acts. 2M. 1 interior. Prod: Theatre Four, New York, 1979.

Vere, a handsome WASP Yalie, returns home after a year in prison to Rudi, his flamboyant, hard-living Puerto Rican lover, and they try to pick up their relationship where they left off. Their agreement was to break all social rules; in Vere's absence, Rudi has been promiscuous, but Vere wants Rudi to be faithful to him. When Vere decides to leave, Rudi pulls a knife; Vere responds by drawing a gun and aiming it at Rudi and then at himself.

Amateur Night at the Baths by Harry H. Long and Joseph Uher. Musical. Full length. 2M. 1 interior.

A two-hour cabaret featuring characters from all aspects of gay life — bookstores, baths, class rooms, offices — who in their own special way bring their truest gay feelings to the fore as examples of "The Gay Lifestyle."

American Hamburger by Robert Heide. Drama. One act. 3M. 1 exterior. $35/$25. Prod: Theatre for the New City, New York, 1976.

A middle-class history teacher who dresses in leather and frequents waterfront bars, a costume freak dressed as George Washington, and Maxwell Bodenheim, the Village poet who was murdered by sailors, meet in Washington Square amidst a drug scene. A poetic imagist piece about the thin line between choosing life against death, being against nothingness.

Angel Honey Baby Darling Dear by Robert Patrick. Comedy. One act. 2M, 2F. 1 interior. Prod: Old Reliable Theatre Tavern, New York, 1970.

Merle Post and Paul Rommell were lovers in Detroit: Merle is the hottest playwright in New York, Paul an attractive drifter. Anne, Merle's mistress, brings Paul home, supposedly to be Merle's editor — in fact, she, like Paul, has tired of Merle's dependency and they plot — unsuccessfully — to get rid of Merle. All of this is watched — and possibly imagined — by the indomitable, irascible Sophie, a maid who never gets to see the high life of the jet set she works for.

Antiphon by Alan Stringer. Drama. One Act. 1M. 1 exterior (repr). Prod: University of New Mexico Experimental Theatre, Albuquerque, 1979.

Night. A young man approaches his lover's door, knocks, receives no answer. He goes to a nearby phone booth, dials and leaves the phone off the hook to ring in his lover's house. To persuade his lover (who is home) to pick up the phone, he talks (through a door vent) about their relationship and various aspects of gay and straight reactions to gayness. The phone ringing stops, signalling the possibility of communication.

Any Woman Can by Jill Posener. Comedy-drama. Full length. 1 interior (repr). Prod: Gay Sweatshop, London, 1976.

From girls' school adolescence to the "meat market" of the gay scene, Ginny becomes a committed lesbian in a heterosexual world, experiencing random compensations and oppressions along the way. She encounters several situations with other women: heterosexual dabbler, female chauvinist pig, timid closet lesbian and passive women who emulate the sexual mores of the straight world.

Apartment on Castro Street, An by N. A. Diaman. Drama. Three acts. 4M. 3 interiors.

The changes and development of four gay men sharing an apartment in a gay neighborhood in San Francisco in the mid-1970's.

GAY THEATRE ALLIANCE

As Time Goes By by Noel Greig and Drew Griffiths. Drama. Three acts. 6M. Prod: Gay Sweatshop, London, 1977.

A three-part historical drama, set in England in 1896, in the aftermath of the Wilde Trials; in Germany, 1929-1934, from the stock market crash to the Night of the Long Knives; and the United States in 1969, at a certain bar on Christopher Street. The play attempts to dramatize the change in consciousness from homosexual to gay.

At Saint Judas's by Henry B. Fuller. Drama. One act. 3M, 1F (+ numerous extras). 1 interior. Publ: in *The Puppet-Booth,* twelve plays by Henry B. Fuller, Century Company, New York, 1896.

Ten minutes before he is to be married, a bridegroom discovers that his best man is in love with him and has been doing everything possible to prevent the marriage. Shocked, the bridegroom forces the best man to kill himself.

Ballad of the Sad Cafe, The by Edward Albee, adapted from the novella by Carson McCullers. Drama. Full length. 14 M, 6F. Unit set. $55/$30. Prod: Martin Beck Theatre, New York, 1963. Publ: Houghton Mifflin, Boston, 1963. Agent: Dramatists Play Service.

Three people in a small Southern town — the proprietor of the Sad Cafe, her jailbird husband and her distant cousin, a hunchbacked dwarf, are in love. The husband loves the wife, the wife loves the dwarf, and the dwarf loves the husband. The wife throws her husband out of her bed on their wedding night, and he returns several years later after being in prison, to find her being attentive to the dwarf, who becomes enamored of the husband.

Baptism, The by LeRoi Jones (Imamu Amiri Baraka). Drama. One act. 4M, 7F. 1 interior. Prod: Writer's Stage Theatre, New York, 1964. Publ: Grove Press, New York, 1967. Agent: Claire S. Degener, Sterling Lord Agency, 75 East 55th Street, New York, N.Y. 10022.

A boy comes to a minister to be baptized, and a homosexual tries to show him that it's pointless. The minister and a group of women try to sacrifice the boy, but a messenger comes to return the boy to The Man.

14   GAY THEATRE ALLIANCE

Barnaby and NewnipPurr by Jeff Dailey. Drama. Two acts. 2M. 1 interior. $50/$25.

Barnaby is off for a month's business on the coast. NewnipPurr is to occupy his vacant apartment. Through NewnipPurr's scheming, the two encounter one another before their scheduled meeting. That scheming wins NewnipPurr a variety of things, including Barnaby's plane ticket to the coast.

Beauty Standards by Sandra deHelen and Kate Kasten. Comedy. One act. 2F. 1 interior. $20/$10.

A dialogue between two women who express the grotesque and self-hating body images that society has taught people to internalize.

Bed, The by Robert Heide. Drama. One act. 2M. 1 interior. $35/$25. Prod: Caffe Cino, New York, 1965.

Two men on a bed when "sex is dead" and "God is dead."

Beneath the Surface by Daniel Curzon. Comedy. One act. 8M, 4F. 1 interior. Negotiable. Prod: Earnest Players, San Francisco, 1979.

Eleven members of the prevailing minorities are trapped together in a subway train underwater. The characters, all representing types (Latino, handicapped woman, gay man, lesbian, white man, et al.) reveal their true feelings toward other minorities. At the end of the play, all of the other characters turn on the Foreigner.

Bent by Martin Sherman. Drama. Two acts. 15M. 4 interiors, 4 exteriors. Prod: Royal Court Theatre, London, 1979. Publ: Avon Books, New York, 1980. Agent: Charles Hunt, Fifi Oscard Associates, Inc. 19 West 44th Street, New York, N.Y. 10036.

In 1934 Berlin, Max and Rudy are two lovers trying to escape the Nazi purge of homosexuals. They flee to several cities and are captured in a forest outside Cologne. Max watches Rudy being killed by guards on the trip to Dachau. In the camp, Max passes for Jewish (wearing a yellow star) rather than gay (a pink triangle) to get better food and treatment. He befriends Horst, a pink triangle, and gets him transferred to his work detail where they gradually become friends and fall in love. Horst becomes ill and Max performs fellatio on an SS guard to get cough medicine for him. He is reported and Horst is forced to electrocute himself on the prison fence. Max wears Horst's pink triangle uniform and also kills himself on the fence.

Berry-Picker, The by James Purdy. Drama. One act. 2M. 1 interior. Publ: in *Out of a Clear Blue Sky,* New London Press, Dallas, Texas, 1980. Agent: Gilbert Parker, Curtis-Brown Ltd., 575 Madison Avenue, New York, N.Y. 10022.

Concerns the relationship of a once-famous hockey star, now a semi-invalid and his youthful idol-worshipping caretaker.

Best Friend by Michael Sawyer. Drama. Full length. 1M, 3F. 1 interior. $50/$35. Prod: Lyceum Theatre, New York, 1976. Publ and Agent: Samuel French.

Carolyn Parsky seems to lead a rich full life; on returning from vacation she wants to share her experiences with Anita. her closest neighbor, who tells her she has become engaged. At first Carolyn seems overjoyed, but she gradually reveals she is an emotional cripple —dependent on life's casual passers-by — and especially dependent on Anita. Carolyn drives off the fiance by maligning Anita to him and Anita believes she's been jilted. But he returns and he and Anita confront Carolyn with the truth.

Birthday by Steven J. Myers. Comedy. One act. 3M, 1F. 2 interiors. Negotiable. Prod: The Glines, New York, 1977.

The Boy has been kept in the nursery for twenty years. He is content, but still not satisfied, for there is something missing. Mother and Father argue over the "surprise" birthday party being given by an anonymous caterer. The caterer arrives and all three find something they need in him, but it is The Boy who is the recipient of the caterer's favors. This birthday is the start of a new life for The Boy as the caterer helps him face his own desires and needs.

Born on Sunday by Frank Holland. Musical drama. Two acts. (Lead sheets available.) 13M, 8F (Doubling). 4 interiors, 2 exteriors.

Gay activists, preparing for the annual New York City parade, discover that liberation is more complex than merely sexual acceptance. Constant outside forces and personal entanglements sidetrack them, while within the organization one faction gains control and is taking the group in a radically dangerous direction.

Boy Bishop, The by Ken Gass. Comedy-drama. Three acts. 13M, 4F (extras). 10 interiors, 4 exteriors. Prod: Factory Lab Theatre, Toronto, 1976. Publ: in *Canadian Theatre Review*, Fall, 1976. Agent: Great North Agency Ltd., 345 Adelaide Street West, Toronto, Ontario M5V 1R5.

In the New France of the late seventeenth century, the governor, bishop and intendant of the colony decide to distract their subjects by staging a Boy Bishop ceremony, in which a young boy substitutes for the bishop for one day. A clever, illegitimate fourteen-year-old who is also gay gets himself selected and decrees that all may take part in an orgy without guilt or punishment. Shortly before his day ends, he decrees that time will stop for one hour so that the people can create a New Order.

Boy Meets Boy by Bill Solly and Donald Ward, music and lyrics by Bill Solly. Musical comedy. Two acts. (Original cast album available.) 8M, 5F (Doubling). 6 interiors, 3 exteriors. Prod: Actor's Playhouse, New York, 1975. Publ: in *Gay Plays*, Avon Books, New York, 1979. Agent: Helen Merrill, 337 West 22nd Street, New York, N.Y. 10011.

In 1936 London, the social event of the season is the forthcoming marriage between two men: predatory American millionaire Clarence Cutler and mousey British aristocrat Guy Rose. But Guy misses his own wedding, becomes romantically involved with world-famous reporter Casey O'Brien and, inspired by love, transforms himself into a dashing heartbreaker. Complications abound, and newly-glamorous Guy finds himself performing onstage at the Paris Folies before love triumphs for a happy ending.

Boys In the Band, The by Mart Crowley. Comedy. Two acts. 9M. 1 interior. $50/$35. Prod: Barr-Wilder-Albee Playwrights Unit, New York, 1968. Publ: Noonday Press, New York, 1968. Agent: Samuel French.

Michael invites friends over to celebrate another friend's birthday. Michael's old straight college roommate calls up in desperation and comes to the party uninvited, and beats up one of the guests. The guest of honor arrives, as does one of his presents, a male hustler. Michael suspects his old roommate is gay and devises a game in which each guest must call the one person he ever really loved. The roommate calls his wife, not the man Michael suspected, leaving Michael submerged in guilt.

Breathing Room by Philip Real. Drama. One act. 2M. 1 interior. Prod: Theatre Rhinoceros, San Francisco, 1977.

Sean and Tony have met in a San Francisco bar and gone to Sean's apartment to spend the night. Sean is an accountant with American Express and Tony is a waiter. In the early hours of the morning, after the two have had sex, the two men begin to get to know each other. Sean presses Tony to see him again, but Tony resists. They quarrel about this and about their attitudes on sex and relationships, discovering they like and respect each other. Tony leaves, making no commitment as to whether he'll return.

Breeders by Bob Ost. Comedy-drama. Three acts. 5M, 3F. 5 interiors, 1 exterior. Negotiable. Prod: Nat Home Theatre, New York, 1979. Agent: Karen Gromis, 157 West 57th Street, Suite 604, New York, N.Y. 10019.

Originally set up by aging sculptor Carl Lindstrom as a protest against overpopulation and the further "immoral" breeding of the species, the Heller Foundation has been corrupted into an insular homosexual community. Here, artist John Mauree and poetess Pat Stark can control their lives, work and young lovers — Chris and Joanne, respectively — until their young lovers discover each other and their latent heterosexuality. Carl's male secretary, Lee Fredericks, also disrupts the colony by trying to help his heterosexual best friend Rick gain admission. Only older artist Rita Jameson understands the full extent of the hypocrisies and prejudices that must ultimately be overcome.

Bring on the Boys by Richard Erickson and Dean McIlnay. Comedy. Two acts. 7M. 1 interior. 5%/gross.

A character study of six gay men and one straight man who share a dressing room during the run of a hit off-Broadway musical in the early 1960's. The play deals with their camaraderie, their bitchiness with each other, and their constant bickering with the straight man, culminating at one point in a fist fight. As the run of the show ends, their deep-seated affection for each other becomes apparent.

GAY THEATRE ALLIANCE

Brussels Sprouts by Larry Kardish. Comedy. Full length. 2M, 1F. 1 interior. Prod: Factory Lab Theatre, Toronto, 1972. Publ: in *The Factory Lab Anthology,* Talonbooks, Vancouver, B.C., 1974. Agent: Great North Agency, 345 Adelaide Street West, Toronto, Ontario, Canada M5V 1R5.

Two young friends take a motorcycle tour of Europe during the summer preceding their first year of college. One of the men feels passionately about and for the other, but the latter is not eager to make sexual contact with his good friend. They get to Brussels: the hotel room is bleak, it is raining. A mysterious but attractive girl visits the room; she is both catalyst and intermediary between the two men.

Butley by Simon Gray. Drama. Full length. 4M, 3F. 1 interior. $50/$35. Prod: Criterion Theatre, London, 1971. Publ: Viking Press, New York, 1972. Agent: Samuel French.

Butley is a university professor who shares his apartment and his office with a former star pupil, Joey, now also a teacher. Butley faces both the ultimate breakdown of his marriage and his relationship with Joey. Butley's painful discoveries are made against a backdrop of petty university politics and unease about student dissent.

Buzzy by Mentha Marley III. Drama. One act. 5M, 1F. 1 interior. Prod: Theatre XII Studio, Inc., New York, 1979.

Michael Lockett, a Broadway dancer, plans a party for his best friend, Gerald Palmer, who arrives early to caution Michael about allowing his ex-lover "Buzzy" to dominate his life and ruin his career. Buzzy arrives at the party with his ex-wife who has had enough of his playing off her sympathies and leaves him to Michael and his own devices. Another guest arrives and Buzzy causes grief to all which eventually leads him to his own self-destruction; unable to cope with his own homosexuality, he takes his own life.

C

Cakes by Richard Ronan. Drama. One act. 9M. 1 interior. Negotiable.

A love-death play in the French tradition; dialogue is in both French and English.

Cakes and Ale by Richard Ronan. Comedy. Two acts. (Tape of music available.) 3M. 1 interior. Negotiable.

Vaudeville for three actors; several satirical vignettes in a framework of a duo in a classic vaudeville show. Soundtrack is used as part of the live dialogue throughout.

Call Me Jacky by Enid Bagnold. Drama. Three acts. 4M, 4F. 1 interior. Prod: Calabash Productions, Oxford, England, 1968. Publ: in *Four Plays,* Little, Brown, Boston, 1971. Agent: Robert A. Freedman, Brandt and Brandt, 1501 Broadway, New York, N.Y. 10036.

An earlier version of **A Matter of Gravity** (q.v.).

Can I Touch You, Mr. Santos? by Ross M. Levine. Drama. Three acts. 9M, 5F (Doubling). 7 interiors (repr).

A university student in Berkeley falls secretly in love with a rich young foreign student from Peru. Neither his girlfriend nor his roommate understands why he remains friends with the Peruvian who seems so selfish and inconsiderate. The student learns that his father is ill; meanwhile, he is writing a play which, although about a man and a woman, is really about his love for the Peruvian. One night they go out drinking and the student misses his plane home, where the father has died during surgery. The student's play is broadcast over radio, and the Peruvian hears it, understanding nothing. Summer break comes, and the student's love for the Peruvian remains unrequited.

Cannibals Just Don't Know No Better by Harvey Fierstein. Satire. Two acts. 1 interior, 1 exterior. 4M, 1F. Agent: Helen Merrill, 337 West 22nd Street, New York, N.Y. 10011.

A tribe of cannibals that live homosexually is shocked when one of their young men claims to be straight.

Caprice by Charles Ludlam. Comedy. Two acts. 3M, 10F. 1 interior. Prod: Ridiculous Theatrical Company, New York, 1976.

The life and times of a mythic gay hero, Claude Caprice, avatar of fashion.

Captive, The by Edouard Bourdet. Drama. Three acts. 3M, 6F. 3 interiors. Prod: Théâtre Femina, Paris, 1926. Publ: Brentano's, New York, 1926.

Irene DeMontcel is loved by Jacques Virieu who remains steadfast to her even though she is involved with Madame d'Aiguines. Because of this emotional involvement, Irene becomes estranged from her father, betrays her sister, and when she sees the woman again a year after their relationship was ended, loses Jacques when he sees that the women are still in love.

Care and Control by Micheline Wandor. Drama. Full length. Prod: Gay Sweatshop, London, 1977.

In the event of contested custody, who is awarded "care and control"? An unmarried editor whose former lover didn't even visit their daughter for a year and a half? An ex-wife whose drunken spouse returns home to scream abuse at her and a feminist friend? A working-class lesbian whose ex-husband can provide neither adequate housing nor supervision for the children? A collectively scripted piece by the women of the Gay Sweatshop, based on transcripts of actual cases, contrasts the legal guardianship of children to the mother's sexual and political freedom.

Caseworker, The by George Whitmore. Drama. Two acts. 3M, 1F. 1 interior. Prod: Playwright's Horizons, New York, 1976.

Ernie, a welfare caseworker, takes in a drifter whom he looks upon as a son. But Bill, the runaway Ernie befriends, rejects his help and, attempting to ignore his homosexuality, marries. Joey, Ernie's roommate, attempts to intervene.

Castro Street by Joel Ensana. Drama. Two acts. 4M, 3F. 3 interiors, 1 exterior (repr). Negotiable. Prod: San Francisco Stock Company, San Francisco, 1976.

A play dealing with the Eureka Valley community in San Francisco that surrounds the intersection of Castro and 18th Streets. It centers on the conflicts and friendships that develop between the middle-class Irish families that traditionally have occupied the area and the gay people who have blossomed there. The characters range from a gay couple and a fag hag to an older Irish woman, covering the whole range of feelings about gays. Settings also include a gay bar: the Elephant Walk.

Catalyst, The by Ronald Duncan. Comedy. Two acts. 1M, 2F. 1 interior. $50/$25. Prod: English Stage Company, London, 1958. Publ and Agent: Samuel French.

Charles' wife discovers that his secretary, who works in their home, is also his mistress. This is too much for her and she confronts the secretary, who goes away, and is missed by both husband and wife. On a return visit, the two women confront each other again and learn that neither loves Charles, but are drawn to each other. Charles is agreeable and the three share an overt menage à trois.

Cecily's Gala, or Sins of the Father by Richard Ronan. Comedy. One act. 5M, 4F (Doubling). 3 interiors. Negotiable.

An expressionist farce on morality and roles.

Chambers by Paul Stephen Lim. Drama. Two acts. 6M, 1F. 1 interior. Negotiable. Prod: Midwest Playwright's Laboratory, Madison, Wisconsin, 1979. Agent: Biff Liff, William Morris Agency, 1350 Avenue of the Americas, New York, N.Y. 10019.

An aging Midwestern playwright returns to the city of his birth, and with the help of an actress, an actor, and his life-long director-producer-friend, stages four scenes from his autobiographical work-in-progress, the ending of which is known only by his friend.

Children Sliding on the Ice by Kenneth Harris. Drama. Three acts. 12M, 1F (Doubling). 4 interiors, 1 exterior.

Three presumed brothers (1 bartender, 1 young gay, 1 bodybuilder) meet to find their father, and to choose who will kill him because he abandoned them as babies. The father is found and the bodybuilder is selected in lottery. Robbie, the young gay, meets the presumed father and likes him, and is confused. Ed, another gay man who loves Robbie, is introduced; the bartender-brother is killed, and in a dream sequence, reveals the truth to Robbie: the bodybuilder-brother is the father, and also a murderer. He is arrested, Robbie and Ed are united, and the presumed father (who had a gay lover in his youth) decides to seek his youthful love again.

Children's Hour, The by Lillian Hellman. Drama. Full length. 2M, 12F. 2 interiors. $35/$25. Prod: Maxine Eliot's Theatre, New York, 1934. Publ: Knopf, New York, 1934. Agent: Dramatists Play Service.

Two women run a school for girls. A malicious student starts a "scandal" about them (that they are lovers), which precipitates tragedy for the women. It is discovered that the student's gossip is made up, but by then irreparable damage has been done.

Children's Mass, The by Frederick Combs. Drama. Two acts. 5M, 2F. 1 interior. Prod: Theatre de Lys, New York, 1973. Agent: Janet Roberts, William Morris Agency, 1350 Avenue of the Americas, New York, N.Y. 10019.

Geoffrey and Jimmy share their loft in Soho in New York with Dutchie, a transvestite. The play deals with their relationships: toward each other and toward two children, one seven, the other eight years old. The children's mother, a downstairs neighbor, is an alcoholic. The three friends find themselves providing the children with the only family they know. Dutchie finds the strain of controlling her drug habit and accepting the responsibilities of a family too much of a challenge, and gets a man she meets to kill her.

Child's Play by Robert Marasco. Melodrama. Full length. 6M, 9 boys. 1 interior. $50/$35. Prod: Royale Theatre, New York, 1970. Publ and Agent: Samuel French.

In a Catholic boys boarding school of 200, the students have become sinister, stealing up and down staircases after hours, torturing more and more of their fellow students and sending pornographic photographs to a crotchety classics professor's dying mother. Pride, envy, jealousy and perverse hate have infected the students and the staff to cause what has been going on.

Chosen, The by Richard Ronan. Drama. One act. 5M (Doubling). 1 interior. Negotiable.

A minimalist/expressionist play, obliquely involving a near-catatonic boy and an older man and the former's self-inflicted religious drive.

Chris by Mark Dunster. Comedy. Seven scenes. 6M, 6F. 4 interiors, 2 exteriors. Publ: Linden Publishers, New York, 1978.

A bisexual's heavy involvements with people of both sexes, including three young Spanish-speaking men.

Clearing in the Forest by James Purdy. Drama. One act. 2M. 1 interior. Prod: Ensemble Studio Theatre, New York, 1978. Publ: Lord John Press, Northridge, CA, 1980. Agent: Gilbert Parker, Curtis Brown Ltd., 575 Madison Avenue, New York, N.Y. 10022.

Two young men have had a deep emotional attachment to one another. The younger man, Gil, attempts to break this relationship which has become too overwhelming by going through an engagement with a young woman. This relationship has been urged on him by his friend, Burk, in a kind of crazy act of destruction for them both.

The play focuses on the young men's final attempt to understand themselves and their predicament, and ends with Gil's suicide.

Close Friends by John Herbert. Drama. One act. 2M. 1 interior. Prod: Forest Hill Chamber Theatre, Toronto, 1974. Publ: in *Some Angry Summer Songs,* Talonbooks, Vancouver, B.C., 1976. Agent: Ellen Neuwald, Inc., 905 West End Avenue, New York, N.Y. 10025.

A man has a fantasy in which he exorcises the memory of his ex-lover. His lover comes to visit him to discuss their relationship as a pretext. The two men become angry, sometimes violent, and the lover threatens the man with a gang of his friends. As they fight near a window, the ex-lover is shot by his gang by mistake. The man's memory of the lover ends.

Clouds, The by Steph Martin. Comedy. One act. 2M. 1 interior.

Burlesque comedy involving two boys who pick each other up in a bar, and go to one's apartment and discover that both are "gay virgins."

Colonial Dudes, The by Martin Bauml Duberman. Comedy-drama. One act. 2M. 1 interior. Negotiable. Prod: Actors Studio, New York, 1969. Publ: in *Best Short Plays of 1973,* Chilton Books, New York, 1973.

An English professor walks out of his office one morning to find a ratty-looking teenager asleep in the corridor. The play is about how two men of different generations and with apparently little in common can manage to discover their underlying sympathy and caring for each other.

Collection, The by Harold Pinter. Drama. One Act. 3M, 1F. 2 interiors. $25/$15. Prod: Aldwych Theatre, London, 1962. Publ: in *Three Plays,* Grove Press, New York, 1962. Agent: Dramatists Play Service.

Harry, an older man, and Bill, a young dress designer, share a house which is disturbed one night by an anonymous phone call and then by a visitor, James, whose wife, Stella, said she had a one-night affair with Bill. James decided he wanted to see him and an attraction-repulsion develops between the two of them. Harry finds this out and casts doubt as to whether the affair ever took place, which reestablishes an uneasy status quo.

DIRECTORY OF GAY PLAYS 25

Comeback by Daniel Curzon, music by Daniel Turner, lyrics by Daniel Curzon and Daniel Turner. Musical. Two acts. (Tape and sheet music available.) 3M, 3F (Doubling). Cabaret setting. Negotiable.

A male cabaret performer plans to make a comeback as a female cabaret performer. The characters are Rosalind Smith and her former self, George Smith, and various people from his/her past and future. When the musical opens, she has already had the sex-change and is deciding whether or not to return to the stage, and the play takes place the moment before she steps on the stage in a new sexual role. She learns to accept her change and that whether male or female, it is the performance that counts.

Coming Out! by Jonathan Katz. Documentary. Two acts. 5M, 5F. 1 repr. Prod: GAA Firehouse, New York, 1972. Publ: Arno Press, New York, 1975. Agent: Raines and Raines, 475 Fifth Avenue, New York, N.Y. 10017.

"A documentary play about gay life and liberation in the U.S.A.," the play features various scenes about gay life: the Stonewall and Snake Pit raids, Willa Cather, Gertrude Stein and Alice Toklas, Horatio Alger, lesbian cross dressers, the Boise, Idaho witch hunt, etc.

Companion Piece by David Csontos. Drama. Two acts. 4M. 1 interior. $50/$35.

A romance concerning four men who lack experience in "getting close."

Confessions of a Female Disorder by Susan Miller. Drama. Two acts. 6M, 8F (Doubling). 4 interiors. Prod: Eugene O'Neill Theatre Center, Waterford, Conn., 1973. Publ: in *Gay Plays*, Avon Books, New York, 1979. Agent: Flora Roberts, 65 East 55th Street, New York, N.Y. 10022.

Ronnie journeys through high school and college to marriage and career and finds herself unhappy being a wife and mother. As she explores what it means to be a person, she becomes a lesbian.

Conpersonas by Paul Stephen Lim. Drama. Two acts. 2M, 2F. 1 interior. $50/$25. Prod: University of Kansas at Kennedy Center, Washington, D.C., 1976. Publ: Samuel French, New York, 1977. Agent: Biff

Liff, William Morris Agency, 1350 Avenue of the Americas, New York, N.Y. 10019.

A Jesuit priest discovers that his identical twin brother, an advertising executive, has just committed suicide, and he tries to relive all the events and relationships that his brother had had — with an older European man, an advertising woman, and the woman's daughter.

Conversations for the Duke and Duchess of Windsor by Cal Yeomans. Drama. One act. 1M, 1F. 1 interior.

A female tries to extract and bolster the nearly vanished masculinity of her spouse.

Cornbury: the Queen's Governor by William M. Hoffman and Anthony Holland. Comedy. Two acts. 8M, 9F (Doubling). 4 interiors, 2 exteriors (repr). Prod: New York Shakespeare Festival Public Theatre, New York, 1976. Publ: in *Gay Plays*, Avon Books, New York, 1979. Agent: Helen Merrill and Helen Harvey, c/o Harvey, 410 West 24th Street, New York, N.Y. 10011.

A documentary satire and "revanchist revisionist history" of Edward Hyde, Viscount Cornbury, transvestite governor of New York colony in 1708, containing historical information of the period as well as historical speculation on the central character.

Country Music by Michael Smith. Comedy. Two acts. 5M, 2F. 1 interior. Prod: Theatre Genesis, New York, 1971. Publ: in *The Off-Off-Broadway Book,* Bobbs-Merrill, Indianapolis, Indiana, 1972.

A group of people pass the winter in an old farmhouse in New England, including a very old man, a young girl, a straight couple and a gay couple. In the spring, the couples have aged considerably, but only physically; they also go through some transformations, including doing a scene from *The Cherry Orchard*.

Couplings and Groupings by Megan Terry. Documentary. One act. Various M, F (Doubling). Prod: Theatre Verité. Publ: Pantheon, New York, 1973. Agent: Elisabeth Marton, 96 Fifth Avenue, New York, N.Y. 10011.

Interviews with a vast cross-section of people — gay, straight, young, old, etc. — concerning personal relationships in the United

States, and their rapidly changing nature. Ordinary people talk of new ways of relating in a composite portrait of flux and uncertainty.

Crimes Against Nature by the Gay Men's Theatre Collective. Documentary. One act. 9M. Prod: San Francisco, 1977.

A collectively created and performed piece, based on the lives of the men of the collective, reflecting their survival techniques as gay men.

C.T.! by Steven J. Myers. Drama. One act. 5M. 1 interior. Negotiable.

Al, Ken, Todd and Mary are gathered at Ken's apartment where Mary is polishing his number for the evening's drag show. The others discuss the merits — or, as Al contends, the disadvantages — of games like the drag number. Ken says that it is not as cruel as the the game that Al's little "straight" friend, Robbie, is into by being a cock-tease. When Robbie arrives to catch a buzz before his date, Ken turns the c.t. game around, with the others joining in. Al learns that some games are more harmful than others.

Curing of Eddie Stoker, The by Lanie Robertson. Comedy. One act. 2M. 1 interior. $30/$20. Prod: Penndragon Productions, Philadelphia, 1975. Agent: Howard Rosenstone and Co., Inc., 850 Seventh Avenue, New York, N.Y. 10019.

Set in the near future, the play is a satirical parody of the psychological "cures" to which homosexuals are subjected. Stoker goes to a psychiatrist because he has "heterosexual tendencies"; the doctor explains that his abnormal condition is unconscionable because the act of procreation has long been forbidden. After tests, the doctor tells him that he is "depraved, degenerate and disgusting," and Eddie is guilt-ridden and contrite. The doctor agrees to "cure" him, so that he can go home to his husband, two dogs and cat as a gayer man.

Daddy Violet by George Birimisa. Satire. One act. 2M, 1F. $20/$15. Prod: Caffe Cino, New York, 1967. Publ: in *Prism International*, University of British Columbia Press, Vancouver, Canada.

Story of three flowers on the side of a mountain overlooking the Mekong Delta during the Vietnam War. One of the violets is gay.

Daddycakes, Daddycakes by Kerry Kammer. Comedy-drama. Two acts. 3M, 2F. 1 interior.

Wayne, a generally drugged-up, unemployed aspiring actor, shows up at Wayne and Sydney Mae's house for the weekend. Daniel, his boyfriend, is a successful middle-aged novelist, and Sydney Mae, his wife, is a writer of children's books. Wayne challenges Sydney Mae for the top spot on Daniel's list of emotional and financial priorities. The play examines the thin lines which divide relationships, marital and otherwise, addressing itself to the question of infringement of relationships upon each other.

DIRECTORY OF GAY PLAYS 29

Dallas! by David Mitchell. Comedy-drama. Two acts. 4M, 4F (Doubling). 1 interior.

People visit Dallas, who is dying. He throws a party to say goodbye.

Dancing for the Kaiser by Andrew Colmar. Drama-comedy. Three acts. 12M, 4F. 6 interiors. Prod: Circle Rep, New York, 1975.

In 1918 London, a member of Parliament publishes a small political scandal sheet that no one reads. Anxious to be in the center of attention, he creates a controversy. He claims that a famous American dancer, Martha Willow, is a lesbian and she and a lesbian friend are planning a production of Wilde's *Salome* to encourage the Cult of the Clitoris in their efforts to assist Germany in the war effort. The dancer sues him in criminal court for libel, and he tries to discredit her.

David and Jonathan by Philip Katz, music by Arie Lishans, lyrics by Philip Katz. Musical. Two acts. (Tape of music available.) 11M, 2F (Doubling). 1 interior, 1 exterior.

A musical version of the Biblical story of David and Jonathan: David wins King Saul's affection and slays Goliath, and Jonathan and David fall in love. When David becomes more popular than Saul, he sees this as a threat and tries to get rid of him. Saul pursues David relentlessly, but David eventually proves to him he is not an enemy. Jonathan is killed in a battle, Saul commits suicide, and David wants to die also. But Jonathan's ghost convinces David to go on, because his nation must be healed.

Day After the Fair, A by James Purdy. Drama. One act. 5M, 1F. 1 interior. Publ: in *Two Plays by James Purdy*, New London Press, Dallas, Texas, 1979. Agent: Gilbert Parker, Curtis Brown Ltd., 575 Madison Avenue, New York, N.Y. 10022.

Two clowns have a long-standing feud with the Clown Master and a hired assassin named Oswin; the clowns are brothers, whose relationship is incestuous and full of ungoverned jealousy for one another. Their relationship is complicated by their association with Oswin and his wife, Elga, with whom they have a close sexual relationship. By hiring Oswin to murder the Clown Master, who has ruined his own career, the older of the two clowns sets off a series of events which end in the destruction of all the characters.

Day Mr. Donald Disappeared, The by S. Michael Schnessel. Comedy. One act. 4M, 5F. 1 interior. Negotiable. Prod: Princeton Community Players, Princeton, N.J., 1979. Publ: *Southern Theatre,* Volume 22, Number 2, Spring, 1979. Agent: Lucianne S. Goldberg, 255 West 84th Street, New York, N.Y. 10024.

On the evening before a political victory dinner, Hilda Matheison waits in a restaurant for her husband, the new mayor. He never appears, nor does his best friend and campaign manager, Art Mingus. Mr. Donald, Hilda's flamboyant and effeminate hairdresser appears briefly and vanishes. So do millions of other people — fully ten percent of the world's population — leaving only their clothes behind. As radio reports point to the obvious conclusion — that all homosexuals have disappeared — Hilda and Lucille Mingus come to a mutual conclusion about their husbands. When Mr. Donald suddenly reappears after a tryst with one of the maids, they understand that appearances are not always what they seem.

Dear Dora/Dangerous Derek: An American Tragedy by Rob Shivers. Drama. One act. 3M, 7F or 10F.

Adapted from the poem "Dear Dora/Dangerous Derek Diesel Dyke" by Freda Smith. Extreme contrasts of one woman's personality to demonstrate the schizophrenic lifestyle society demands.

Dear Love of Comrades, The by Noel Greig and Drew Griffiths, music by Alex Harding. Drama. Full length. 5M. Prod: Gay Sweatshop, London, 1979.

Based on the letters, diaries and writings of Edward Carpenter and three men he was intimately involved with, the play is set in Sheffield from 1891 to 1899. It examines in detail men's changing emotional and sexual relationships with one another and the intense political activity in which they were engaged.

DIRECTORY OF GAY PLAYS 31

Death and Resurrection of Mr. Roche, The by Thomas Kilroy. Comedy. Three acts. 6M. 1 interior. Prod: Olympia Theatre, Dublin, 1968. Publ: Faber and Faber, London, 1969. Agent: Margaret Ramsay Ltd., 14a Goodwins Court, London WC2, England.

On a Saturday night in Dublin, a group of men are drinking together all evening, including a man recently returned to the group after being married, a gay man, and a medical student. One of them, Mr. Roche, has a seizure and dies and the men agree to dispose of the body. As they are doing so, he mysteriously returns to life (or is he a ghost?) to try to convince another man of his own vitality.

December to May by Jane Staab. Romance. Two acts. 2M, 4F. 2 interiors. $35/$20. Prod: Playwright's Horizons, New York, 1977.

A love story betwen two women: a man's wife confronts his mistress; they become friends and fall in love. The man survives the loss of both women with some difficulty. The women choose each other in their new discovery of themselves without much difficulty.

Degrees by George Birimisa. Comedy. One act. 2M, 1F. 1 interior. $15/$10. Prod: Theatre Genesis, New York, 1966.

A doctor and his young lover are in conflict: the doctor is very Establishment and conservative; the young lover is on the verge of becoming a hippie.

Delightful Bonus, A by Carmine J. Buono. Comedy. One Act. 1M, 3F. 1 interior.

A man turns to homosexuality after five years of marriage. His wife wants to save the marriage and asks her neighbor, a sex therapist, to help. The neighbor is interested in the husband herself and agrees to help. The man's mother also tries to save the marriage, but eventually the couple has a serious talk and the wife accepts the reality of the ending marriage.

Demons by Daniel Curzon. Comedy-drama. Three acts. 1M, 3F (Doubling). 1 interior. Negotiable.

A man is examining his life and is visited by three female visions, representing three phases of his life. The first demon is a nun, representing the religion he was taught as a child. The second demon is his mother, representing his upbringing during his adolescent years. The final demon is his ex-wife, representing his attempt to be straight.

Design for Living by Noel Coward. Comedy. Three acts. 6M, 4F. 3 interiors. $50/$25. Prod: Ethel Barrymore Theatre, New York, 1933. Publ: Doubleday, New York, 1933. Agent: Samuel French.

Menage a trois between Gilda, living in Paris, Otto, a painter, and Leo, a successful playwright. After having an affair with both of them, she goes off with Ernest, marries him and becomes a successful New York decorator. Eighteen months later, Otto and Leo come to get her, and bored with her conventional life, she goes with them.

Diaghilev and Nijinsky (Loves of the Artists, Part II) by Robert Patrick. Comedy. One act. 2M. 1 interior. Publ: in *Mercy Drop and Other Plays*, Calamus Books, New York, 1980.

Diaghilev, ballet entrepreneur, is busy; Nijinsky, his skitzy dancer lover, wants to play.

Diane (Goddess of the Hunt) by R. Fenkel. Political Satire. One act. 2M, 1F. 2 exteriors. Negotiable.

The play concerns the election of a mayor of San Francisco — based roughly on the career of Diane Feinstein. The candidate is created in the early 1960's by a young hairdresser, who after the assassinations of Harvey Milk and Mayor Moscone, has greatly matured and realizes that he has helped to create an ambitious, greedy political figure who must be destroyed, or uncreated. She is a symbol for all the political figures today who don't hear their constituents, especially gays. (Diane may be played by a man in drag.)

Doubles by John Arnold. Drama-comedy. One act. 2M. 1 interior. Prod: California Playwrights Festival, Sacramento, CA, 1978.

Afte five years, ex-lovers meet for drinks at the Top of the Mark in San Francisco. Uneasy small talk turns into a bittersweet reunion.

Downtown Local by C .D. Arnold. Drama. One act. 4M. 1 interior. $15/$10. Prod: Theatre Rhinoceros, San Francisco, 1979.

Four gay men meet in a late night winter subway station: Dennis, an alien from Oregon; Orlando, a New York City Puerto Rican; Vesper, a magical creature floating between Bellevue and the rest of the world; and Georgie, Vesper's protector. They are all waiting for the downtown local, their dreams and each other amidst the trash and the express trains rumbling through.

Drag, The by Mae West. Drama. Three acts. Prod: Bridgeport, Conn., 1927.

The son of a well-known, conservative judge is gay and has married the daughter of a doctor interested in sexual "diseases" (like homosexuality) to avoid dealing with his gayness. He falls in love with a straight man who is in love with his wife. The son's ex-lover comes to the wife's father to be cured; when the doctor has no cure, he murders his ex-lover, and his father covers up the murder by calling it suicide.

Dress Made of Diamonds, A by George Birimisa. Drama. Full length. Various M, F. Numerous interiors, exteriors (repr). $15/$10. Prod: Matrix Theatre, Hollywood, CA, 1976.

The first seventeen years of Joey's life.

Drop In the Pudding, A by Paul Vanase. Drama. Two acts. 9M, 1F (Doubling). Abstract set. $50/$20. Prod: The Glines, New York, 1976.

A series of semi-abstract episodes dealing with One, the central character in a search for love. One remains self-centered and childish throughout, while having sexual encounters with The Seductress, The Financial Keeper, The Best Friend, The Stud and The Masochist. One is unwilling to commit himself to any one of the characters so he is left alone, revealing that the self-centered individual in search of love isn't going to find it.

Druce by Mark Dunster. Comedy. Three acts. 8M, 3F. Publ: Linden Publishers, New York, 1976.

A comedy about straight and gay sex on the college scene, involving both teachers and students.

Edward II by Bertolt Brecht, assimilated from Marlowe. Drama. Full length. 16M, 1F (Doubling). Interiors, exteriors. $50/$35. Publ and Agent: Samuel French.

The plot outline of Marlowe's play is simplified, motives altered, and made into an historical ballad. Edward and Gaveston's relationship is made more overtly homosexual. (See next entry.)

Edward II by Christopher Marlowe. Drama. Full length. 26M, 2F (Doubling). Prod: Pembroke's Men, London, 1593. Publ: Avon Books, New York, 1974.

By favoring Gaveston, Edward alienates his lords, the church and his wife. War breaks out and Edward is captured by Mortimer and eventually killed. Edward's son then has Mortimer hanged and imprisons the Queen in the Tower.

Elagabalus by Martin Bauml Duberman. Drama. One act. 4M, 4F. 1 interior. Negotiable. Prod: New Dramatists, New York, 1973. Publ: in *Male Armor: Selected Plays 1968-1974,* Dutton, New York, 1975.

The story of the androgynous Roman emperor, Elagabalus, but transposed to a contemporary context. "Adrian," 21 years old, heir of a wealthy political family, persists in pursuing his own multipersonnae, sexual and temperamental; he does so in the face of familial/social disapproval — and, ultimately, to the point of defiant suicide.

Electric Map, The by Martin Bauml Duberman. Drama. One act. 2M. 1 interior. Negotiable. Prod: Tambellini's Gate Theatre, New York, 1970. Publ: in *The Memory Bank,* Dial Press, New York, 1970.

The play takes place "backstage" at the famed Electric Map of the battle of Gettysburg. Against that fratricidal struggle, a contemporary fratricidal struggle between two brothers is played out — the older brother attempting to drive the younger (who "operates" the Electric Map) out of town after his homosexuality has been publicly discovered.

Enclave, The by Arthur Laurents. Drama. Full length. 6M, 3F. 1 interior. $50/$25. Prod: Theatre Four, New York, 1973. Publ and Agent: Dramatists Play Service.

A group of congenial friends have restored several adjoining houses in one of New York's more attractive neighborhoods and plan to move in en masse. One of their number, a confirmed bachelor, has resolved to tell the others of the fact of his long-concealed homosexuality, and to bring his young lover as a permanent addition to the group. Although they have always prided themselves on their tolerance, they are outraged, and the enclave itself is periled.

End of the Parade by Stuart Kingsley. Drama. Two acts. 7M. 1 exterior.

The pathos of an individual who has been used by a lover, set against a gay power parade on the Fourth of July.

Entertaining Mr. Sloane by Joe Orton. Drama. Three acts. 3M, 1F. 1 interior. $50/$35. Prod: New Arts Theatre, London, 1964. Publ: in *Gay Plays,* Avon Books, New York, 1979. Agent: Margaret Ramsey Limited, 14A Goodwin's Court, St. Martins Lane, London WC2N 4L1, England.

Sloane comes to a rundown area in search of a room, and after a landlady gives him one, she seduces him. Her brother discovers this, and seduces Sloane himself. Their father believes he saw Sloane murder someone, so Sloane murders the father to silence him. The brother and sister then decide that each may keep Sloane for him/her-self six months of the year.

Ergo by Jakov Lind. Comedy. 13 scenes. 8M, 2F (extras). 4 interiors, 2 exteriors. Prod: New York Shakespeare Festival Public Theatre, New York, 1968. Publ: Hill and Wang, New York, 1968. Agent: Joan Daves, 45 East 49th Street, New York, New York 10017.

An absurdist, fantastical play set in 1905 Vienna, and including Arnulf, "a rather pretty, sensuous boy, dressed in the latest of the latest" who "of course is queer but we enjoy his open happy smile and easygoing way" and his younger brother, Arnold, who uses powder, lipstick and eyeshadow.

Evening with George Sand, An by Milli Janz. Documentary. Full length. 1F.

With music by Frederick Chopin, a collection of the author's work adapted for stage presentation.

Examen, The by Nicholas A. Patricca. Drama. Two acts. 7M (Doubling). 3 interiors. Negotiable. Prod: Victory Gardens Theatre, Chicago, 1980.

Nicholas d'Lallo is unexpectedly elected Pope. Using the examen (his special spiritual discipline), he follows various policies he believes necessary for the institutional Church, and incurs the enmity of powerful Churchmen who want to undermine his projects and discredit him. His chief antagonist tries to blackmail him by revealing his "homosexual affair" with an American priest, and Nicolas' personal and political crises both reach a head. He decides to enact his own identity in the face of both personal and institutional risk.

Experiment in Lust, An by Ross MacLean. Drama. One act. 1M, 1F. 1 interior. $10/$10. Prod: Deja Vu Coffeehouse, Hollywood, 1979.

A clinical, impersonal dissection of human and spiritual values as portrayed though the sexual act. Could be performed by a same-sex couple, though this is not necessary. The play addresses itself to conditions of alienate behavior which should be familiar to a gay mentality.

Faggot, The by Al Carmines. Musical. Two acts. (Sheet music available.) 9M, 5F (Doubling). 1 interior (repr). Prod: Judson Poets Theatre, New York, 1973.

    A musical revue with scenes on various aspects of gay life: bars, movie theatres, hustlers, fag hags, Gertrude Stein and Alice B. Toklas, Oscar Wilde, etc.

Fairy Tales by Harry H. Long and Joseph Uher. Comedy-drama. Full length. 2M. 1 interior.

    Subtitled "Stuff for 2 Faggots to do in Front of an Audience," it is a collection of myths from sources as varied as ancient mythology and contemporary sociology, including handsome princes, evil trolls and the history of fairy magic, presented in the classic fairy tale format.

Family Business by Dick Goldberg. Drama. Full length. 6M. 1 interior. $50/$35. Prod: Astor Place Theatre, New York, 1978. Publ and Agent: Dramatists Play Service.

An old, rich, ailing man dominates the lives of his four sons, three of whom still live at home. He blames them for the death of his wife, and knowing he is about to die, writes a will that closely controls the disposition of his large estate. Each of the sons has an interest in the money: one is heavily in debt, another wants to maintain the family business, the third wants things the way they used to be, and the fourth, gay, son wants to achieve independence from the others.

Fefu and Her Friends by Maria Irene Fornes. Drama. Three acts. 8F. 4 interiors, 1 exterior. Prod: New York Theatre Strategy, New York, 1977. Publ: in *Performing Arts Journal,* Winter, 1978. Agent: Bertha Case, 42 West 53rd Street, New York, N.Y. 10019.

In 1935 New England, a woman asks seven of her friends to her country home for a day-long visit. The play examines each of the women and their inter-relationships; at one time, two of the women had been lovers.

Final Exams by Ken Eulo. Drama. Two acts. 2M. 1 interior. $75/$40. Prod: Courtyard Playhouse, New York, 1977. Agent: Helen Harvey, 410 West 24th Street, New York, N.Y. 10011.

David and Michael face their final exams, and the examining of themselves and their relationship as well. David now realizes that Michael has taken over his personality, and rules him in almost everything he does. David feels trapped. When he confronts Michael with the facts, Michael denies David's feelings. The play ends with David making one final effort to rid himself of Michael.

Find Your Way Home by John Hopkins. Drama. Three acts. 3M, 1F. 1 interior. $50/$35. Prod: Open Space Theatre, London, 1970. Publ: Samuel French, New York, 1975. Agent: William Morris Agency, 1350 Avenue of the Americas, New York, N.Y. 10019.

Julian is joined at his apartment by Alan, his middle-aged lover, who has decided to leave his wife and children to live with Julian. They are confronted by Alan's wife, who is shocked and outraged. The two of them have an intense discussion, ruthlessly dissecting their marriage. By the end of the play, Alan has not made a final decision either way.

DIRECTORY OF GAY PLAYS

First Breeze of Summer, The by Leslie Lee. Drama. Full length. 8M, 6F. 1 interior. $50/$35. Prod: St. Mark's Playhouse, New York, 1975. Publ and Agent: Samuel French.

The story of a middle-class black family in a small Northeastern city: the father owns a plastering business and runs it with one of his sons; his other son, about to graduate from high school, wants to be a doctor or scientist. The father's mother comes to visit, and in flashbacks, recalls her life. The younger son worships her, and she helps him with his problems, and with accepting his blackness and his homosexuality.

First Lover by Susie Chancey. Musical. Two acts. 6F. Negotiable. Prod: Cambridge Lesbian Theatre, Cambridge, MA, 1979.

Defined as a lesbian play and subtitled "The Anti-Death-Culture Scream," the play moves in spiralling scenes through five phases of being: introduction, Cambridge, childhood, coming out and carrying on. Its issues include dreams, class, marriage, lesbianism (practice and herstory), ritual, children and revolution.

Flatbush Tosca by Harvey Fierstein. Musical satire. Two acts. (Sheet music available.) 3M, 1F, 2 drags. 3 interiors, 1 exterior. $50/$35. Prod: New York Theatre Ensemble, New York, 1975. Agent: Helen Merrill, 337 West 22nd Street, New York, N.Y. 10011.

In this adaptation of the Puccini opera, Tosca is a drag queen, Cavaradosi a drug dealer and the villain, Scarpia, a black police chief. It roughly follows the opera plot, including scenes sung in the original Italian.

Fog by Robert Patrick. Drama. One act. 2M. 1 exterior. Prod: Old Reliable Tavern, New York, 1969.

Stud and Fag meet in a freak fog in Central Park. Each tired of the limits of their roles, they take advantage of the complete lack of vision to pretend they are each other. But Fag gets wise and uses the darkness to get from Stud what he wants.

Forever After by Doric Wilson. Comedy. One act. 2M, 2F (and/or drag). 1 interior. $40/$35. Agent: Terry Helbing, 51 West 4th Street, Room 300, New York, N.Y. 10012.

A romantic comedy, theatrically stylized. The muses of tragedy and comedy come down from the theatre's proscenium to interfere in the relationship of two male lovers. The muses can be played by women or impersonators.

Forever Faithful by Carmine J. Buono. Black comedy. One act. 2M, 1F. 1 interior.

Tiny Gelson, a lonely artist who weighs about 300 pounds and lives by himself in a small cluttered studio, has just won a nice sum of money in a supermarket bingo contest, and wants to alleviate his frustrating existence. On a recommendation from a friend, he contacts a call boy service to have a hustler sent to him. The hustler was driven to the job by a girlfriend, unaware that he hustles; she is pregnant and wants an abortion. Tiny wants the hustler to spend the night, simply for affection. When he leaves the next morning, Tiny decides to go on a diet, feeling more positive about the world.

Fortune and Men's Eyes by John Herbert. Drama. Full length. 6M. 1 interior. $50/$25. Prod: Actors Playhouse, New York, 1967. Publ: Grove Press, New York, 1967. Agent: Samuel French.

A youth is thrown in jail and tells a "queen faggot" and a tough bunkmate, who have victimized an innocent black youth, that he "is not queer." When the tough subjugates him in the shower room, the youth becomes a "homosexual tyrant," beating up the tough and the black youth, who says he wants friendship. After a Christmas party, the black youth is attacked again and sent to solitary.

Four Play by Ross MacLean. Comedy. One act. 2M, 2F. 2 interiors. $10/$10. Prod: Los Angeles Actor's Theatre, 1977.

Two married couples having affairs amongst themselves, in every possible combination. Four bisexual people fatally in love with themselves and trying to find someone else who agrees.

Fourtune by Bill Russell, music by Ronald Melrose, lyrics by Bill Russell. Musical. Two acts. (Demo tape available.) 2M, 2F. 3 interiors.

DIRECTORY OF GAY PLAYS   41

Fourtune is the name of a pop group—two male and female couples—who are touring after their first album is released. In the course of the play, the four people regroup into gay couples.

Freaky Pussy by Harvey Fierstein. Comedy. One act. 9M, most drag. 1 interior. $50/$35. Prod: New York Theatre Ensemble, 1974. Agent: Helen Merrill, 337 West 22nd Street, New York, N.Y. 10011.

A group of drag-prostitutes are chased from their home (a subway men's room) when it is turned into a chic nightclub.

Fred and Harold by Robert Patrick. Slapstick. One act. 2M. 1 interior. Prod: Old Reliable Theatre Tavern, 1969. Publ: in *Robert Patrick's Cheep Theatricks,* Samuel French, New York, 1975. Agent: Samuel French.

Fred wants to make it; Harold doesn't (but Harold really does); do they?

Freddie Corvo Show, The by Emily L. Sisley. Comedy. One act. 5M, 3F. 1 interior. Prod: The Glines, New York, 1977. Agent: Helen Merrill, 337 West 22nd Street, New York, N.Y. 10011.

In the setting of a TV talk show, host Freddie Corvo somewhat reluctantly explores "gay is good." The invited celebrities emerge from the closet just as vain, argumentative, scared, whacked-out and hard to deal with as straight people are. Thus the theme: neither best nor better, just equally *good.*

Friday Night Dances by Steph Martin. Musical. Two acts. 8M, 4W. 1 interior.

Friday night in New York as a backdrop to how straight people see gays and how gays see each other. "Boy meets boy," plus a chorus of 4 men and 4 women who represent "the community."

Fugue In a Nursery by Harvey Fierstein. Comedy with music. One act. (Sheet music or tape available.) 3M, 1F. 2 interiors. $50/$35. Prod: La Mama E.T.C., New York, 1979. Agent: Helen Merrill, 337 West 22nd Street, New York, N.Y. 10011

Part Two of the Torch Song Trilogy: two couples, one straight and one gay, spend a weekend together in bed.

Game of Fools by James (Barr) Fugate. Drama. Two acts. 14M, 4F (extras). 6 interiors, 1 exterior. Publ: One, Inc., Los Angeles, 1954.

In the 1950's four gay men who go to school together have agreed to meet once a month to explore their gayness. On their last meeting, they are arrested on trumped up charges of sodomy so that a Mayor can get reelected on a clean-up campaign. Three plead guilty and one innocent. All are sent to prison for thirteen months and when they're released, one joins a monastery and another slits his throat. When the other two meet for a reunion four years later, one has gone into banking and plans to marry and the other has gone to Europe in his father's business, where he has found tolerance and freedom. When their visit is interrupted by detectives sent by one of the four's hysterical mother, the two decide to stay instead of returning to Europe, to fight prejudice and provide an example for other gay men.

Gemini by Albert Innaurato. Comedy. Two acts. 4M, 3F. 1 exterior. $50/$35. Prod: Circle Rep, New York, 1977. Publ: James T. White, New York, 1978. Agent: Dramatists Play Service.

In the backyard of adjoining houses in the poorer sections of South Philadelphia, it is the eve of Francis' twenty-first birthday, and he is visited by two college friends who set up their tent in the backyard. The friends brother and sister, are wealthy, attractive and from upper class backgrounds, which contrasts with Francis' surroundings. The sister is in love with Francis, but he is infatuated with her brother.

Gentle My Love by Bob Cernos. Drama. One act. 2M. 1 interior. Negotiable.

Abe has brought a young macho-type boy, Billy, to his studio apartment on the lower east side of New York. Abe, fiftyish, is a survivor of the Warsaw uprising and concentration camps, where he experienced homosexual love, but not sex. He has left his wife and children to find this love again. Billy gets into the relationship to relieve the pressure of his relationship with his virgin girlfriend, and for financial reasons, afraid to admit he might be gay. As the two begin to reveal their feelings, love begins to bind them together.

Georgie Porgie by George Birimisa. Drama. Full-length. 16M (Doubling). Various interiors and exteriors (repr). $30/$25. Prod: Village Arena Theatre, New York, 1971. Publ: in *More Plays From Off-Off-Broadway,* Bobbs Merrill, Indianapolis, 1971.

The rise and fall of Georgie.

Gethsemane Springs by Harvey Perr. Drama. Two acts. 5M, 6F. 2 interiors. Prod: Mark Taper Forum, Los Angeles, 1977. Agent: Flora Roberts, 65 East 55th Street, Suite 702, New York, N.Y. 10022.

A prismatic look at an hour or so in the lives of eleven characters who are gathered for a weekend at a country estate. The central character, Marianne, is involved in a menage à trois with her husband of twenty years and a charismatic gay man who has brought along several of his lovers, past and present, for the weekend.

Gilles de Rais by William M. Hoffman. Melodrama. Three acts. 10M, 5F (Doubling). 1 interior/exterior (repr). Prod: New York Theatre Strategy, New York, 1975. Agent: Helen Merrill, 337 West 22nd Street, New York, N.Y. 10011.

The life and times of the historical Bluebeard. The leader of Joan of Arc's victorious armies, the richest man in France, a connoisseur of

44   GAY THEATRE ALLIANCE

all the arts, an alchemist, Gilles de Rais was put on trial in 1440 for heresy and the murder of at least 200 young boys.

Girls In the Band, The by Angela Pescatore. Musical Comedy. One act. (Tape available.) 8F (Doubling). 1 interior.

Set in a Manhattan discotheque with a church-like atmosphere, the play centers on a naive young go-go dancer from New Jersey and her admiration for the lead singer of the rock group.

Golden Pyramids at Ohama by Rochelle Holt Dubois. Comedy. One act. 1 exterior. Prod: International Women Writer's Conference, Goucher College, Maryland, 1977.

A mythical endeavor with emphasis on the Egyptian goddesses and their relationships to each other.

Good-bye Pompeii by Robert Wallace. Comedy-drama. Two acts. 4M, 3F. 1 interior. Prod: Theatre Glendon, Toronto, 1977. Agent: Ralph Zimmerman, Great North Agency Limited, 345 Adelaide Street West, Suite 500, Toronto, M5V 1R5.

At the end of a school term, five people who have been sharing a house together for that school year re-examine their relationships. One of the men ended a relationship with one of the women and is now involved with one of his female teachers; another man and woman are still involved; a third man has come out and has brought a man home with him on the roommates' last evening in the house.

Good Night, Cookie Lavagetto by Coleman Morrison. Comedy. Three acts. 4M, 8F. 3 interiors.

In a stereotype reversal, two gay men are portrayed with all the characteristics usually attributed to straights (stability, professionalism, discriminate, etc.) while the straight people around them have all the characteristics usually attributed to stereotyped gays (promiscuity, neurotic, untrustworthy, etc.).

Goodnight, I Love You by William M. Hoffman. Comedy-drama. One act. 1M, 1F. 1 interior. Prod: Caffe Cino, New York, 1964. Agent: Helen Merrill, 337 West 22nd Street, New York, N.Y. 10011.

A young gay man, Alex, chats on the telephone late one summer night to his best friend, a young straight woman, Lisa. Alex believes he is losing his lover. He desperately searches with Lisa for ways to keep Tom and begins to fantasize what it would be like to be pregnant by him. The friends soon believe in the fantasy until they both become aware that their own relationship is based on illusion — that Alex will someday make love to Lisa.

Great Nebula in Orion, The by Lanford Wilson. Drama. One act. 2F. 1 interior. $15. Prod: Stables Theatre Club, Manchester, England, 1971. Publ and Agent: Dramatists Play Service.

The chance meeting, after many years, of two girlhood friends. One has married well, and the other has a successful career, but her female lover left her. Their conversation reveals the emptiness and longings in their lives.

Green Bay Tree, The by Mordaunt Shairp. Drama. Three acts. 4M, 1F. 2 interiors. Prod: London, 1932. Publ: Allen and Unwin, London, 1933.

Julian Dulcimer is now in his early twenties. When he was eight, he was adopted (bought) from his natural father by Mr. Dulcimer, who has raised the boy as a mirror of himself — a "complete dilettante" in a life of "exquisite luxury." Julian has fallen in love with, and wishes to marry, Leonora, a clear-headed working woman. Mr. Dulcimer, angry and jealous, cuts off Julian's allowance. Julian, attempting to break from Mr. Dulcimer, returns to his natural father, who, when he realizes that Dulcimer stands in the way of his son's marriage, kills Dulcimer. Julian renounces Leonora and returns to himself and Mr. Dulcimer's way of life.

Green Shutters by Elizabeth Addyman and June Wyndham Davies. Drama. Three acts. 7M, 3F. 2 interiors. Prod: Arthur Brough Players, Folkestone, England, 1963. Publ and Agent: English Theatre Guild Ltd., London, 1964.

Gervase Hood was the most popular man at Harvard and now a famous author, who surrounds himself with young men to help and serve him. One such man's daughter is in love with Gervase's current assistant. When Gervase is murdered, both she and the assistant confess to protect each other, but when the true murderer is found, the assistant admits he is still taken up with Gervase and cannot reciprocate her love.

Gulp! by John Glines and Steven Greco, music by John Glines, lyrics by John Glines and Robin Jones. Musical farce. Two acts. (Tape of music available.) 6M. 1 exterior. Negotiable. Prod: The Glines, New York, 1977. Publ: in *Blueboy*, January-February (Act One) and March (Act Two), 1979.

A reluctantly gay lifeguard, an infatuated Hunter College bookworm, a rotund, outrageous matchmaker with a lover who is Mr. Butch Construction Worker and two other equally outlandish characters meet on the beach at Coney Island.

Guttman Ordinary Scale, The by Martin Bauml Duberman. Comedy. One act. 3M, 1F. 1 interior. Negotiable. Prod: New Dramatists, New York, 1972. Publ: in *The Gay Alternative*, Issue No. 9, 1975.

In the laboratory of a leading sex researcher, a young, goofy college student presents himself for "testing." What follows is a Marx-Brothers-like farce in which all traditional standards of testing and sexual "norms" are turned on their heads.

Hacking It by Wallace Hamilton. Comedy. Two acts. 4M, 1F. 1 interior. Agent: Robert Freedman, Brandt and Brandt, 1501 Broadway, New York, N.Y. 10036.

 Colter Johns, a closeted gay and head of New York sales for his family's business, is confronted with his neurotic lover, Jerry, who has decided to leave, his soon-to-be-divorced brother, Winston, and his niece, Lara, who has come to New York to live with her boyfriend, but lives with Colter instead. Jerry returns, finds Lara, retreats to a hotel and picks up a trick. Colter goes after him and finds him with his trick. Colter finally gets himself out of the closet.

Happy New Era by Paul Hunter. Comedy. One act. 1M, 1F. 1 interior. $15. Prod: The Glines, New York, 1977.

 A man and his wife, in their early forties spend an agonizing New Year's Eve trying to adjust to the news that their college freshman son is gay. Since their son is happily adjusted to the fact, the couple realizes it's their problem and work through it to an eventual reconciliation with their son.

48 GAY THEATRE ALLIANCE

Harry and Larry by Richard Taylor. Drama. Two acts. 2M. 3 interiors. Negotiable. Prod: 18th Street Playhouse, New York, 1978. Agent: Patty Dobbins, Connecticut Talent Corporation, 300 Central Park West, New York, N.Y. 10024.

What begins as a casual encounter in a library quickly leads to a confrontation between two diametrically opposed personalities, in which one character, Harry, explores, then exploits for his own sense of identity and dominance, the passive and neurotically self-centered Larry, who by the end of the play is not only his captive, but his victim.

Haunted Host, The by Robert Patrick. Melodrama. Two acts. 2M. 1 interior. $50/$25. Prod: Caffe Cino, New York, 1964. Publ: in *Robert Patrick's Cheep Theatricks,* Samuel French, New York, 1975. Agent: Samuel French.

Jay's dead love, Ed, haunts the house. A bitchy friend sends over a straight boy who looks like the lover; Jay falls into the same mutually opportunistic relationship with Frank that he had with Ed, but exorcises both the dead and living boy and faces life alone.

Haverly by Barry Griggs (book, music and lyrics). Musical. Two acts. (Sheet music and tape available.) 9M. 5 interiors, 1 exterior.

Chris, newly arrived in New York, is seeking a career in the theatre. He soon meets Brad, and they begin a relationship. Chris is accepted as a chorus boy in a drag review run by Fred, who's ever at odds with his star performer and other half, Dolly. Eventually Dolly and Fred break up and Chris is compelled to assume Dolly's drag role in rehearsal. Dolly and Fred are reunited in time for the opening of the review.

Headmaster by Mark McHenry. Full length.

The headmaster of a private boys' school launches a one-man purge to rid the school of reputed homosexuals — and snares one boy who isn't gay.

Here's To the Morrow by Robert Lynn Kazmayer. Drama. Two acts. 2M. 1 interior. Negotiable.

Two former high school chums meet in a motel room. Reg is now a traveling salesman trying to support a wife and child. Tim has been bumming around and sometimes living by hustling. During an evening of drinking, Reg is forced to face up to the inadequacy of his married life and the fact that the bond he once had with Tim was stronger than it will ever be with his wife. In the morning, Tim fails in his effort to get Reg to give up his family responsibilities; but Tim has awakened something in Reg that will not soon be quieted.

Hippolytos by Richard Ronan. Drama. Two acts. 10M, 5F (Doubling). 1 interior. Negotiable.

An involved expressionist marriage of the Hippolytos/Phaedra/Theseus legend with Oriental myth.

Home Again Home Again Jiggity Jig! by Sandra Scoppetone. Drama. Three acts. 1M, 3F. 1 interior. Prod: TOSOS Theatre Company, New York, 1974. Agent: Gloria Safier, 667 Madison Avenue, New York, N.Y. 10021.

A lesbian comes home for Christmas and has to deal with her father's reaction to her gayness.

Homerica: A Trilogy on Sexual Liberation by Paul Stephen Lim. Drama. Three acts. 8M, 5F. 3 interiors. Negotiable. Prod: University of Kansas, Lawrence, Kansas, 1977. Agent: Biff Liff, William Morris Agency, 1350 Avenue of the Americas, New York, N.Y. 10019.

The play traces sexual mores in America — past (Victorian and repressed), present (wild and abandoned) and future (bizarre) — by following the history of a basement in New York. It is first used as an antiquarian bookstore, then a single's club, then a travel agency cum hospital clinic.

Hosanna by Michel Tremblay. Drama. Two acts. 2M. 1 interior. Prod: Le Theatre de Quat'Sous, Montreal, Quebec, 1973. Publ: Talonbooks, Vancouver, B.C., 1974. Agent: John Goodwin, 3823 Melrose Avenue, Montreal, Quebec H4A 2S3.

Hosanna, a transvestite, shares a shabby studio apartment with her leatherman lover, Cuirette, with whom she has a stormy relationship. After being horribly humiliated at a Halloween costume ball and contest, she decides to give up the accoutrements of female impersonation.

GAY THEATRE ALLIANCE

Hostage, The by Brendan Behan. Comedy. Full length. 11M, 7F. Various interiors, exteriors. $50/$25. Prod: Theatre Royal, London, 1958. Publ: Grove Press, New York, 1965. Agent: Samuel French.

An innocent British soldier is taken into a bawdy Irish bar by the IRA as a hostage, to be shot if the British execute an IRA youth. He has a romance with a barmaid, who with several of the bar patrons, tries to help him escape. The patrons include Princess Grace, Rio Rita and Mr. Mulleady, three "queers" who sing "We're here because we're queer/Because we're queer we're here."

Hot Rock Hotel by Christopher Caine. Comedy. Two acts. 17M, 2F. 1 interior, 1 exterior. Prod: Truck and Warehouse Theatre, New York, 1978.

On Memorial Day Weekend, the first weekend of the tourist season, numerous confrontations occur among the guests of a gay hotel: some get their suitcases switched, a straight couple wins a weekend trip there, not realizing it's a gay hotel, etc. The guests include an ex-porno star, a politician, a baseball player, a writer and his young boyfriend, and the owner and his friend who helps him run the hotel.

How Are You, Johnnie by Philip King. Mystery. Three acts. 4M, 2F. 1 interior. Prod: Vaudeville Theatre, London, 1963. Publ and Agent: Samuel French (London).

In working-class London, Johnnie Leigh is visited at home by a friend from work and then by a police detective, who wants him to report his friend at work for being "queer." Johnnie finds out that the detective's later "special duty" is seeing a prostitute and enraged, the detective attacks him with a fireplace poker. In the ensuing struggle, the detective trips and falls on the poker and dies; panicked, Johnnie tries to escape.

How I Became a Shadow by James Purdy. Drama. One act. 2M. 1 exterior. Publ: in *Out of a Clear Blue Sky*, New London Press, Dallas, Texas, 1980. Agent: Gilbert Parker, Curtis Brown Ltd., 575 Madison Avenue, New York, N.Y. 10022.

Concerns the relationship between a seventeen-year-old Mexican boy and his overbearing and sadistic cousin, who forces the boy to give up his pet fighting-cock to be entered in the cockfight. The younger boy, through a ruse, murders his persecutor, and becomes an outlaw "like a shadow" in the "defiles of the mountains."

Hustlers by A. J. Kronengold. Comedy. Two acts. 6M, 3F. 2 interiors, 1 exterior. Prod: Cherry Lane Theatre, New York, 1975.

A study of the hustler scene in New York City during a 72-hour period, taking place primarily on Eighth Avenue, the hustlers' district.

Hymen and Carbuncle by Robert Patrick. Comedy. One act. 2M. 1 interior. Prod: Dove Company, New York, 1970. Publ: in *Mercy Drop and Other Plays,* Calamus Books, New York, 1980.

In "Love of the Artists, Part III," Hymen and Carbuncle are rock stars, but Carbuncle's contribution is largely personal; he resorts to manipulative teasing in order to inspire Hymen to greater things.

I

I Saw a Monkey by Randolph Carter. Comedy-drama. One act. 1M. 1 interior. Negotiable. Prod: Cherry Lane Theatre, New York, 1968.

Larry is an appealing youngster of seventeen, whose affair with a wealthy older man is ending because the man's wife is returning from Europe. Through the medium of a farewell letter and phone calls to several former friends and a hostile relative in his home town, his somewhat desperate life and situation are revealed. At the last moment, a possible solution presents itself, and Larry moves on.

Immoralist, The by Ruth and Augustus Goetz, based on the novel by Andre Gide. Drama. Full length. 7M, 2F. 2 interiors, 1 exterior. $50/$25. Prod: Royale Theatre, New York, 1954. Publ and Agent: Dramatists Play Service.

A scrupulous and pleasant young man marries a neighborhood girl in desperation in an attempt to escape the memory of his "abominable crime" of a scandal at school when he was eleven. They move to a village in North Africa, where he becomes fascinated by the young men there. When the wife discovers that she is pregnant, she returns home, and the young man follows her.

DIRECTORY OF GAY PLAYS   53

In a Garden of Cucumbers by Cal Yeomans. Tragi-comedy. One act. 4M. 1 interior. Prod: Theatre Atlanta Studio, Atlanta, GA, 1969.

Set in a small town in Florida a few years back, for two transvestite performers and two studs. The plot concerns what happens to two lonely and horny old women who suddenly find 1,000 National Guard Troopers camping out for one night in the city park across from their house.

In Celebration Of by Steven J. Myers. Tragi-comedy. One act. 4M, 2F. 1 interior. Negotiable.

Four friends gather to celebrate Etienne's good fortune and see him off as he embarks on his chosen career. The gay character in the play, he seems to them the "undependable fag"; why is he the one meeting success? He has good fortune, opportunity and talent and takes advantage of these gifts. He is flamboyant and assertive, offering his friends this philosophy, and as he leaves, they remain behind with their dreams, ignoring the ideas he offers.

In Gay Company by Fred Silver. Musical revue. Two acts. 4M, 1F. 1 interior. Prod: Little Hippodrome Theatre, New York, 1974. Publ: Genesis III Music Corporation, 170 Northeast 33rd Street, Ft. Lauderdale, Fla. 33334.

Musical revue, with little spoken dialogue, satirizing society's attitudes toward male homosexuality, including numbers about Sheridan Square, cruising, dancing, YMCA, and relationships. Videotape of performance available at Lincoln Center Library for the Performing Arts.

Increased Occupancy by Robert Heide. Drama. One act. 4M. 1 interior. $35/$25. Prod: New York Theatre Strategy, New York, 1978.

Two painters' private domain is threatened by a maniacal obsessed landlord and then invaded by an ominous exterminator. The artists are driven to a brutal act to sustain their "art." The territorial oppressiveness of the landlord incites the tenants to assault him thus sacrificing himself, and the persistent plea for recognition of the exterminator causes only ambivalence in the artists, who prefer to remain focused on their work.

GAY THEATRE ALLIANCE

Indiscreet by Roger Baker and Drew Griffiths. Drama. Full length. 4M. 1 interior. Prod: Gay Sweatshop, London, 1976.

The continuing story of ex-***Mister X*** (q.v.) who drifts partially back into the closet. After an object lesson in oppression, he "sings" because he's "Glad to be Gay."

International Stud, The by Harvey Fierstein. Comedy with music. One act. 2M, 1F. 1 interior. $50/$35. Prod: La Mama E.T.C., New York, 1978. Publ: in *Gaysweek Arts and Letters*, July 10, 1978. Agent: Helen Merrill, 337 West 22nd Street, New York, N.Y. 10011.

Part One of the "Torch Song Trilogy": love story between a female impersonator and a bisexual who meet at a backroom bar in New York City.

Invitation to a Bear-Baiting by Wallace Hamilton. Drama. Two acts. 5M. 1 interior. Agent: Robert Freedman, Brandt and Brandt, 1501 Broadway, New York, N.Y. 10036.

Wesley Stuart, a gay in his early fifties who is assistant manager of an antique gallery, finds that his alcoholism is standing in the way of his appointment as manager of the gallery. He has a lover in his twenties who aspires to be a professional guitarist and singer, and fails in his first public performance. Out of these two failures a bond of determined survival is forged.

It Swings, Julian by Richard Gray. Drama. One act. 2M.

A man uses his playful fantasy to solidly and quietly freshen his relationship with his lover.

J

Jerusalem Thorn, The by Ramon Delgado. Drama. Two acts. 2M, 1F. 1 interior. $50/$35. Prod: Acting Wing, Inc., New York, 1979.

    A gay artist in Owensboro, Kentucky, who has worked on *Gone with the Wind,* resists the efforts of his friend, a younger high school art instructor, to have the artist's dying dog put to sleep. The artist's sister threatens their relationship if he will not sell the family property to some Arabs and split the profits with her. The art instructor has been fired and has come to say goodbye, but the artist, seeing him as a replacement for a recently deceased longtime companion, is reluctant to give up hopes for a similar relationship with the art instructor.

Jimmie by Robert Esposito. Drama. One act. 2M. 1 interior. Prod: Triad Playwrights.

    James, an aging homosexual, has been given his eviction notice. He has lived in this "room" for almost thirty years. He spends his last moments with Roscoe, the superintendent, his ex-lover, and with Zinca Milanov.

GAY THEATRE ALLIANCE

Jingle Ball, The by Drew Griffiths. Musical. Full length. 3M, 5F. 1 interior. Prod: Gay Sweatshop, London, 1976.

Collectively devised by the Gay Sweatshop, The Ugly Sisters are a drag act. Cinders and Buttons are their stage management. Cinders meets Miss Charming, a theatrical impresario; with the help of the Lavender Fairy she decides to zap the Jingle Ball! A feminist panto. With songs by Jill Posener, Tom Robinson and Michael Richmond.

Joyce Dynel by Robert Patrick. Musical. Two acts. 16M, 7F (Doubling). Unit set. $50/$25. Prod: Old Reliable Theatre Tavern, New York, 1969. Publ: in *Robert Patrick's Cheep Theatricks,* Samuel French, New York, 1975. Agent: Samuel French.

A poet loves a Catholic boy; the boy loves Mary Magdalene (big time gossip columnist); Mary loves a weightlifter; the weightlifter loves fame. It's all interwoven by the poet into a Christmas entertainment: the life of Christ.

Jungle of Cities by Bertolt Brecht. Drama. Full length. 11M, 4F (extras). Various interiors, exteriors. $50/$35. Publ and Agent: Samuel French.

Set in Chicago, a savage battle is waged between two men, whose relationship is both homosexual and sadomasochistic. The action, which takes place over a period of three years, goes from a lending library in Chicago to a deserted railroad worker's tent in the gravel pits by Lake Michigan.

Killing of Sister George, The by Frank Marcus. Comedy. Three acts. 4F. 1 interior. $50/$25. Prod: Bristol Old Vic, Theatre Royal, London, 1965. Publ: in *Gay Plays,* Avon Books, New York, 1979. Agent: Samuel French.

Sister George is a famous character in a BBC soap opera, a nurse who does good deeds and spreads cheer. Because of bad ratings and because of the gossip about her personal life, the BBC decides to "kill her off" by getting her in a truck accident. The woman who comes to tell her is pleased to see that the gossip is true, for she finds the cigar-smoking, gin-drinking, hard-cursing Sister George waited on slavishly by a female lover — whom the woman promptly proceeds to steal from her.

Kiss the Sky by Lane Bateman. Drama. Three acts. 7M. 1 interior.

A teacher and his black lover return from a Halloween party in costume with several friends (one of whom is blind), to find one of the teacher's students from a previous university at their home. He has run away from his parents. His father trails him and enters in the midst of a campy party, embarrassing the teacher. When his son refuses to leave with him, the father returns a few hours later and shoots his son and the teacher.

Kitchen Duty by Victor Bumbalo. Comedy. One act. 3M. 1 interior. Negotiable. Prod: The Glines, New York, 1979.

Bob, who recently broke up with his lover, goes home with Michael, who's into leather. During their scene, Michael handcuffs and manacles Bob, but Bob doesn't like it and asks to be freed. Michael has the keys to the equipment in his leather jacket, which he lent to a friend. Bob gets hysterical and has an asthma attack, and Gary, his ex-lover, must bring him medicine from his upstairs apartment. Conservative Gary finds the situation perverse. The confrontations of the three explore the nature and roles of gay relationships.

L

Last Resort, The by Ralph Carideo. Musical. Full length. 4M, 1F.

The love relationship between a gay man and a bisexual man is explored.

Late Snow, A by Jane Chambers. Comedy. Two acts. 5F. 1 interior. Negotiable. Prod: Playwright's Horizons, New York, 1974. Publ: in *Gay Plays*, Avon Books, New York, 1979. Agent: Gloria Safier, 667 Madison Avenue, New York, N.Y. 10021.

Five women are snowbound in an isolated cabin: Ellie, a college professor; Perfect Peggy, Ellie's first lover; Pat, an antique dealer, Ellie's last lover; Quincey, a college student, Ellie's current lover; and Margo, a novelist, Ellie's next lover.

Latent Heterosexual, The by Paddy Chayefsky. Comedy. Two acts. 9M, 3F. 3 interiors. Publ: Random House, New York, 1967. Agent: Robert Sanford, 234 West 44th Street, New York, N.Y. 10036.

John Marley, an extremely successful forty-year-old author, is set in his ways and quite happy as a well-adjusted homosexual, whose only problem is that he is paying too much in taxes. He consults his accountants who propose a twofold solution: incorporation and marriage. He then discovers that he is falling in love with the woman that he marries.

Leather Man, The by Hans Eppendorfer. Docu-drama. One act. 2M. 1 interior. Negotiable. Prod: Lucernaire Forum Theatre, Paris, 1979.

Subtitled "Hans Eppendorfer Speaks with Hubert Fichte," a series of actual interviews between the journalist Hubert Fichte and Eppendorfer, an outspoken homosexual rights activist in West Germany, the play fuses autobiographical and fictional material to create an archetypal character in three stages: alienated manchild as murderer/prisoner; "reintegrated" professional as successful editor of a gay cultural review; programmed hedonist as "the Leather Man." At each stage the irony of each "adjustment" emerges and the search for tenderness in an oppressive society must go on.

Legacy, The by George Whitmore. Drama. One act. 3F. 1 interior. Prod: The Fourth "E", New York, 1979.

Alva, a famous sculptress, falls ill on her tour of the United States. While she recuperates, Flora, an old friend, brings her her legacy from a former teacher of hers — all of her letters unopened.

Lesbian Play for Lucy, A by Eleanor Hakim, music by Tamara Bliss. Musical. Two acts. (Sheet music available.) 3F. Various interiors, exteriors (repr). $50/$35. Prod: Medusa's Revenge Theatre, New York, 1978.

A Lesbian Play for Lucy explores the eternal triangle of that Mother-Daughter-Sister trinity of archetypes through the myth of Demeter/Hecate and Persephone in conjunction with that of Athena. This is enacted within an experimental format that draws upon classical and modern traditions of drama, opera and music theatre, as well as upon American vaudeville and 1930's and '40's movie musicals.

Lesson Number One by Joel Ensana. Drama. One act. 2M. 1 interior. Negotiable.

A play about the need of people for other people: the loneliness of an ex-prizefighter — now old — and a gay social worker, who like all the others in the prizefighter's life, uses him. The prizefighter lets him, out of desperation to learn and for attention.

60 GAY THEATRE ALLIANCE

Little Murders by Jules Feiffer. Comedy. Full length. 6M, 2F. 1 interior. $50/$25. Prod: Broadhurst Theatre, New York, 1967. Publ: Random House, New York, 1968. Agent: Samuel French.

The study of a modern metropolitan family, consisting of a matriarchal mother, a milquetoast father, a sister, and a brother who's trying to adapt himself to homosexuality. The sister wants to marry, and she and her fiance try to find a preacher to marry them who won't use the word "God." After they succeed, the sister is killed by a sniper's bullet. A detective with many "unsolved crimes" tries to determine the "subtle pattern" that is forming.

Long Shots by Larry Glaister. Dramatic Comedy. Two acts. 3M, 1F. 1 interior. $50/$25.

Greg, from Wisconsin and a student at NYU, and Ray, a window dresser and native New Yorker, are lovers. Greg's parents come to New York City for a visit, and the two men plan to conceal their relationship while they visit, but are unable to do so because their picture appears on the front page of the *New York Times* as part of Gay Pride Week coverage. The parents discover the relationship and the play examines parental adjustment to gay identity and the strength of all these relationships.

Lord Alfred's Lover by Eric Bentley. Historical drama. Two acts. 20M, 2F (Doubling). Unit set. Negotiable. Prod: The Hippodrome, Gainesville, Florida, 1979. Publ: in *Canadian Theatre Review*, Spring, 1978.

The old story of the Oscar Wilde trials (1895) told and seen in a new way — specifically, through the eyes of Lord Alfred Douglas shortly before his death in 1945.

Love Letters by Rochelle Holt Dubois. Drama. One act. 15F + chorus/dancers (Doubling). Minimal set.

A series of love letters between women, set in a dream of a fantasy forest, where women create messages of love and whispering sensuous invitations to the women they come in contact with, have memories of or desires of renewing their relationships.

Love Match by Richard Hall. Dramatic comedy. Two acts. 3M, 3F. 2 interiors. $50/$35. Prod: The Glines, New York, 1977. Agent: Warren

DIRECTORY OF GAY PLAYS 61

Bayless, Curtis Brown Ltd., 575 Madison Avenue, New York, N.Y. 10022.

A Hollywood star decides to make a film about a gay athlete, and runs into opposition from his wife, his agent and the gay writer of the novel on which the film will be based.

Lovers by Peter del Valle, music by Steven Sterner, lyrics by Peter del Valle. Musical revue. One act. (Score available.) 6M. Prod: TOSOS Theatre Company, New York, 1974.

An examination of gay love relationships through three male couples, essentially satiric in style.

Loving Friends by Joseph Gath. Drama. Three acts. 3M, 1F. 1 interior. Prod: Turtle Bay Music School, Turtle Bay, New York, 1978.

On opening night for Mark's first play, he goes to pick up his parents and Kevin, a would-be actor shows up and is met by Phillip, Mark's roommate of 20 years and one-time lover. Phillip tries to make Kevin because he thinks the two are having an affair. Mark's mother arrives alone, and sees that Kevin might be a threat to Phillip and Mark and asks him to leave. Sonia and Mark discover that their relationships with their mates are similar, and Mark realizes that love without sex is is better than sex without love.

Ludwig and Wagner by Robert Patrick. Comedy. One act. 2M. 1 interior. Publ: in *Mercy Drop and Other Plays,* Calamus Books, New York, 1980.

In "Loves of the Artists, Part I," Wagner, the greatest composer, attempts to flee his royal lover, Ludwig of Bavaria: but how do you skip town when your boyfriend is an absolute monarch?

Lying in State by Lane Bateman. Comedy-drama. Three acts. 4M, 4F. 1 interior. Prod: JFK Center for the Performing Arts, Washington, D.C., 1974.

Two gay men and two gay women pretend to be married in order to qualify for "married-student housing" at a university. One of the women's parents arrive unexpectedly and are met by the ex-lover of one of the men, and that man and his current lover break up. The ex-lover tries to get the two men to reconcile, and the two men reach an amiable parting of the ways.

Madness of Lady Bright, The by Lanford Wilson. Comedy-drama. One act. 2M, 1F. 1 interior. $15. Prod: Caffe Cino, New York, 1964. Publ: in *Gay Plays,* Avon Books, New York, 1979. Agent: Dramatists Play Service.

Leslie Bright is a fortyish homosexual gradually disintegrating in his room one hot Saturday afternoon. He vainly tries to contact friends, but can only reach American Airlines and Dial-a-Prayer. He covers a range of emotions as he addresses himself in the mirror, facing facts about the men who've signed their names over his bed. Two other people play various roles and parts of Leslie's nature, and sometimes his inner torment, which is alleviated by a descent into madness.

Malcolm by Edward Albee, adapted from the novel by James Purdy. Drama. Full length. 16M, 7F (Doubling). Various interiors, exteriors. $50/$25. Prod: Shubert Theatre, New York, 1966. Publ: Atheneum, New York, 1966. Agent: Dramatists Play Service.

A fifteen-year-old boy, well dressed and well spoken, has been sitting daily on a park bench in front of a hotel. He is seen by an elderly astrologer who speaks to him one day and discovers that he is waiting for his father, who has disappeared. The man takes psychological dominance over him and sends him on a series of visits to various couples and finally to a blonde pop singer, who kills him with drink and sex.

Many Loves by William Carlos Williams. Drama. Three acts. 13M, 12F (Doubling). 1 interior. Prod: Living Theatre, New York, 1959. Publ: New Directions, New York, 1961. Agent: New Directions, 80 Eighth Avenue, New York, N.Y. 10011.

As a "counter-play" to three unrelated sequences on love, a young man, author of the three short pieces, needs to get an older man, who is in love with him, to finance the production of his play, without concessions. The playwright is in love with and about to marry his leading lady, and tries to conceal this from his backer.

Marriage à la Mode by Graham Jackson. Comedy. One act. 2M, 2F. 3 interiors (simultaneous). $25/$10. Prod: Victoria University Dramatic Club, Toronto, 1971.

Vera and Andrew have been married for four years. They have recently been investigating their homosexual potential and like it enough to "elope" with a member of their own sex, without telling each other. Confrontation is engineered by the two people with whom they're eloping and most of the play's action centers on Vera and Andrew's attempts to avoid telling the truth to one another.

Marry Me! Marry Me! by Dennis R. Andersen. Comedy. Two acts. 5M, 3F. 2 interiors. Prod: Barr-Wilder-Albee Workshop. Agent: One Star Ltd., 1501 Broadway, New York, N.Y. 10036.

Mr. and Mrs. Whittaker face the graduation of their unpredictable daughter and the marriage of their conventional son. But, much to everyone's surprise, the daughter becomes engaged to the most conventional fiance imaginable, and the son runs away with the best man at his wedding. The mother and father come to some unusual conclusions about their own relationship in the process.

Martha's Boy by Ludmilla Bollow. Drama. One act. 2M, 1F. 1 interior. $10. Prod: St. Louis, Missouri, 1969.

Aunt Mable's middle-aged mundane life of housework and bingo suddenly opens up when her artistic nephew moves in, introducing her to the world of the arts: plays, concerts, etc. Today he reveals he'll be moving, and Mable must decide whether loving him includes accepting his newly revealed homosexuality.

Matter of Gravity, A by Enid Bagnold. Comedy. Full length. 4M, 4F. 1 interior. $50/$35. Prod: Broadhurst Theatre, New York, 1976. Publ and Agent: Samuel French.

Mrs. Basil lives in a decaying English country house with a lesbian, alcoholic cook and is visited by her grandson from Oxford and his friends: a lesbian left-wing philosopher and her girl friend, a polished fiftyish homosexual and his somewhat hysterical young boy friend. The grandson proposes to the lesbian's girl friend and she accepts because she covets the estate. After spending several years in Jamaica, the two return with two children and Mrs. Basil turns over the estate to them and joins her cook as an inmate in a nearby asylum.

Maurice and Harold by Jim Lee. Drama. Four acts. 2M, 2F. 6 interiors, 4 exteriors. Agent: Mrs. E. Robertson, 106-24 Ditmars Blvd., East Elmhurst, N.Y. 11369.

Four people live in Atlanta in a closed world of people seeking to be free, sexually and spiritually. Maurice, Harold, Renee, and Michelle are tennis players who find themselves drawn toward each other's dedication to the game and winning. Each feels constrained because he or she cannot be part of the society they wish. Harold and Renee are both light-skinned blacks, who are shunned by their ethnic group because they can pass for white. The two women stage a party to try to lure Maurice and Harold for the night, but succeed only in drawing the men closer together.

Maurice Galba by Gerald Ray Williams. Drama. One act. 2M. 1 interior. $25/$15. Prod: University of Oklahoma, Norman, Oklahoma, 1978.

Maurice Galba, a reclusive billionaire, once a leading silent film legend, finally breaks decades of silence and agrees to meet with a young Hollywood interviewer who wants to do his biography. Galba, confined to a wheelchair after years of rejuvenation treatments, watches his old films, and seeing one with the journalist, begins to tell stories of Hollywood before sound — they are comic, bizarre, lurid, and/or homoerotic. Galba knows "the truth" about every major scandal, usually from participation in the murders, rapes and homosexual orgies with other big-name stars. The journalist gets him to agree to further interviews, so that he can set up Galba film showings, talk show appearances, etc.

Mercy Drop by Robert Patrick. Drama. Two acts. 1M, 2F (Doubling). 1 interior. Prod: W.P.A. Theatre, New York, 1973. Publ: In *Mercy Drop and Other Plays,* Calamus Books, New York, 1980.

Johnny Baxter is taking acid and walking through a set of scenarios written by playwright Marvin Partridge; the purpose? To change Johnny's head and help him leave his "drop-out" world and return to normalcy. In the process, we learn that Johnny and Marvin are lovers — and that it is Johnny forcing Marvin to help him get away: "Make me stop loving you, Marvin," he has ordered.

Metaphors by Martin Bauml Duberman. Drama. One act. 2M. 1 interior. Negotiable. Prod: Cafe Au Go Go, New York, 1968. Publ: in *Collision Course,* Random House, New York, 1968.

An eighteen-year-old applies for admission as a freshman to Yale. He and the Interviewer, a middle-aged man of traditional views (the young man's decidedly are *not*), perform a series of startling jousts and confrontations.

Miss Stanwyck Is Still In Hiding by Larry Puchall and Reigh Hagen. Comedy-drama. Two acts. 6M, 2F. 1 interior. Negotiable. Prod: Drama Committee, New York, 1979. Publ: Act One, Scene One in *Blueboy,* February, 1980.

Don and Brian are lovers whose lives are disrupted when Don, a child psychiatrist, comes out during a television interview and gets fired as a result. This causes conflict in their relationship as Don considers becoming an activist to get some kind of "stardom," to the annoyance of Brian, a cynical, apolitical film magazine writer. Don's fantasy of writing The Great American Novel also puts the two at odds. Both men mature and resolidify their relationship on more realistic grounds.

Mister Jello by George Birimisa. Comedy. One act. 4M, 1F. No set. $25/$20. Prod: Playbox, 1968.

A drag queen enters as a straight man and slowly transforms to his nightclub outfit, for his job at the Club 69; a social worker is in a

66 GAY THEATRE ALLIANCE

freezing, rat-infested apartment in Bedford-Stuyvesant; a hippie wants to plant a tree in Astor Place; a prostitute in black leather whips Mr. Jello. They all live in their own worlds, but end up as the family in *Death of a Salesman*.

Mister Jones: A Dramatic Interludes by Louie Crew. Comedy. One act. 9M, 3F (Doubling). 1 interior. $10/$2. Publ: in *GPU News,* Vol. 4 No. 8, June 1975.

In a dramatic montage, family figures, bunny girls, drunk fraternity collegians, and a clown doubling as an authoritarian dean tromp in and out of the main dialogue between an interracial gay male couple. Short enough to play as a break between acts of a longer show, and can play in front of a main curtain.

Mister X by Drew Griffiths and and Roger Baker. Drama. Full length. 4M. Prod: Gay Sweatshop, London, 1975.

Based on the pamphlet *With Downcast Eyes* by Andrew Hodges and David Hutter, the play presents in a simple style the problems encountered by all gay men before they come out.

Model by Douglas Derek Roome. Drama. One act. 3M. 1 interior. Negotiable. Publ: Scene Two in *Gay Literature,* Summer, 1975.

A character study of a pedophile and two boys, one imaginary and one real.

Month of Fridays, A by Wallace Hamilton. Comedy. Two acts. 4M. 1 interior. Prod: Lambda Theatre Group, New York, 1973. Agent: Robert Freedman, Brandt and Brandt, 1501 Broadway, New York, N.Y. 10036.

Ben, a gay welfare executive in his thirties, has been emotionally frosted by the frigidities of gay life in New York. "Bad enough to be gay," he complains, "without being human, too." With the aid of a former lover, Vincent; a current lover, Chris; and a talkative upstairs neighbor, Chuck, Ben is finally restored to the human race.

Motorcycles by Mark Dunster. Comedy. Full length. 12M, 2F. 6 interiors. Publ: Linden Publishers, New York, 1978.

Motorcycle men who are gay and their relationships seen from the perspectives of New York business, private, parental and female influences.

Movin' Up by Sebastian Stuart. Comedy. One act. 3M, 3F. 1 interior. $25/$10. Prod: No Smoking Playhouse, New York, 1979.

The story of four applicants for a "glamorous, exciting and high-paying" job. One is Chipper Jones, a young gay man from Wisconsin.

Muse, The by Richard Gray. Drama. One act. 2F.

One woman breaks through a relentless depression of her lover with a story she tells.

My Fat Friend by Charles Laurence. Comedy. Full length. 3M, 1F. 1 interior. $50/$35. Prod: Brooks-Atkinson Theatre, New York, 1974. Publ and Agent: Samuel French.

Vicky, a bookshop owner, is overweight, and suffers the slings and arrows of the two people who share the apartment above the store: a young Scottish boy who works as an *au pair,* and a middle-aged homosexual. When a handsome man comes to the store, she is determined to become slim, with her two friends' help. She does so, only to discover that it is her rotundity the man found attractive. She is consoled (up to a point) by her gay friend.

My One and Only You by Ralph Carideo. Comedy. Full length. 4M, 2F.

The play examines the tangled relationships between a gay couple and a straight couple.

N

Naomi Court by Michael Sawyer. Drama. Full length. 3M, 2F. Unit set. $50/$35. Prod: Manhattan Theatre Club, New York, 1974. Publ and Agent: Samuel French.

    Two tenants remain in an apartment house slated for demolition: Miss Dugan, a lonely middle-aged spinster, and David, a fortyish homosexual recluse. After he helps her prepare for a pre-nuptial party for a non-existent fiance, David, driven out by his loneliness, brings home a young hustler. In a series of terrifying scenes, the hustler physically and mentally tortures him. As the hustler leans out the window looking for David's car, David pushes him out to his death.

Nasty Rumors and Final Remarks by Susan Miller. Drama. Two acts. 3M, 4F. 3 interior (unit). Prod: New York Shakespeare Festival, Public Theatre, 1979. Agent: Flora Roberts, 65 East 55th Street, New York, N.Y. 10022.

    A woman falls into a coma and through flashbacks, examines her relationships with her female lover, male lover, best female friend, and one of her children, while in the present, these same people gather in a hospital sitting room to await word on her condition.

DIRECTORY OF GAY PLAYS 69

Nearly All There by Dennis Pearlstein. Drama. Two acts. 10M, 2F. 2 interiors.

The play concerns a love relationship of forty years taking place in an old-age home exclusively for homosexuals. Phillip and Wilfred had originally been teacher and pupil, but ten years later, they met in New York cafe society and became lifetime lovers. The younger man feels he is far too young and healthy to be in an old-age home.

Ned by Mark Dunster. Comedy. Three acts. 11M, 4F. 2 interiors, 1 exterior. Publ: Linden Publishers, New York, 1973.

A dark comedy touching on various aspects of gay, bisexual and straight relationships, set in a college scene.

Nelson Americana by Ross MacLean. Satire. One act. 4M, 1F. 1 interior. $10. Prod: Deja Vu Coffeehouse, Hollywood, 1976.

An update of the American Family, traditional to today's standards: Ozzie is hard at work building bombs in the basement workshop; son David, working hard at becoming a crooked lawyer, is buying drugs from his minority classmate, who molests otherwise innocent drag-queen "son" Rick in the family bathroom. It is up to stalwart mother, Harriet, to simplify the complex situations life presents.

News Boy by Arch Brown. Comedy-drama. Two acts. 6M, 1F. 1 interior. $50/$35. Prod: The Glines, New York, 1979. Agent: Terry Helbing, 51 West 4th Street, New York, N.Y. 10012.

A young man comes to visit an old college friend in New York whom he knows to be gay; he meets the friend's roommate instead, and they have a long discussion about their lives, and the young man admits to being gay. After the two become lovers, the young man's father decides to run for State Senator and tries to get his son to make a public announcement to dispel the rumors about his sexuality that would hurt the father's chances of getting elected.

Night Visitors, The by Richard Hall. Drama. One act. 4M. 1 interior. $50/$35. Agent: Warren Bayless, Curtis Brown Ltd., 575 Madison Avenue, New York, N.Y. 10022.

Two men, lovers, live in the country and are visited by some locals intent on violence and sex. Eventually one of them realizes that his own evasions about his homosexuality have led to the night visit of the men intent on mayhem.

Nightride by Lee Barton. Drama. Two acts. 5M. 1 interior. $25. Prod: Van Dam Theatre, New York, 1971.

A has-been Pulitzer Prize writer is trying to stay off the booze and come to terms with his younger lover in Puerto Rico. He is approached by his agent and a young, openly gay rock singer to use some old poetry as song lyrics, and to let his name be openly associated with the project. The struggle between the older man's unwillingness to come out and the younger man's attempts to make him see the changing times — and responsibilities — form the plot of the play. A relationship the singer has with a strange, mute young man complicates the action.

Nitty Gritty, The or Getting Hitched in Brooklyn Heights by Raymond Banacki. Farce. Two acts. 6M, 1F. 1 interior.

Phillip Fletcher isn't particularly into the gay scene, but at a house party, meets Buddy Boyle and is very attracted to him and the two fall in love, and are convinced they don't want to hide it from anybody. Phillip tells a friend, so that he will tell Buddy's mother, and although he doesn't cooperate, she finds out anyway. The two men want to have a gay marriage and Phillip's friend and Buddy's mother try to prevent it. They foil their countermeasures and emerge victorious.

No Deposit No Return by Robert Wallace. Drama. Two acts. 6M. 1 interior. Prod: WSDG Theatre, New York, 1975. Agent: Great North Agency Limited, 345 Adelaide Street West, Toronto, Ontario M5V 1R5.

Five men, trapped in the Sheridan Square washroom of the downtown IRT subway in New York City, strip away their masks and deceptions to reveal the people they really are.

Nobody Is Here Right Now by Laury Ann Gottesfeld. Drama-comedy. Three acts. 4M, 3F. 1 interior.

In a family in a small town on the East Coast in 1955, one son is gay and one daughter is autistic yet responds to sung questions and speaks her objective truth in sarcastic imagery. A chirpingly naive and friendly sailor enters the picture, and mother, son and another daughter become infatuated with him. The play depicts the hypocrisy of the antihomosexual activity of the time and the oppression of women.

Noon by Terrence McNally. Farce. One act. 3M, 2F. 1 interior. $20/$10. Prod: Henry Miller Theatre, New York, 1968. Publ: Random House, New York, 1968. Agent: Samuel French.

A jokester who never appears has invited a group of people to a loft for a fun afternoon. There is a virgin male, a homosexual, a nymphomaniacal housewife, and a pair of sadists, complete with leather, whips and chains.

Norman, Is That You? by Ron Clark and Sam Bobrick. Comedy. Full length. 3M, 2F. 1 interior. $50/$25. Prod: Lyceum Theatre, New York, 1970. Publ and Agent: Samuel French.

A dry cleaner from Ohio comes to New York after his wife runs away with his brother to discover that his son is gay and is living with another man. He tries to "cure" his son by fixing him up with a prostitute, but she fails and her pride is hurt. Eventually, the wife decides to return to her husband and the two "adopt" their son and his lover.

Now She Dances! by Doric Wilson. Drama. Two acts. 4M, 3F. 1 exterior. $60/$45. Prod: (one act) Caffe Cino, New York, 1961; (two act) TOSOS Theatre Company, New York, 1975. Agent: Terry Helbing, 51 West 4th Street, Room 300, New York, N.Y. 10012.

A multi-leveled, theatrically stylized study of homophobia. Oscar Wilde's *Salome* as played by some of the characters of *The Importance of Being Earnest* turns into a comic/chilling nightmare trial of a liberated, contemporary gay male.

Office Murders, The by Martin Fox. Comedy-drama. Full length. 3M, 1F. 1 interior. Prod: Quaigh Theatre, New York, 1979.

Howard is the publisher of a small magazine, and Jack is his managing editor, who hires Maury, an openly gay male, as an office temp. Jack has left his wife, and Howard admits to having slept with other men, and says everyone knows that Jack has always been gay. He agrees to move to L.A. as Howard's lover and assistant at a new company, and the two agree to kill Howard's wife, and make it look like suicide.

On the Bridge of Time by Richard James Henry. Drama. One act. 2M. 3 interiors. $30/$20.

A white man and a black man meet at a porno movie house and leave together after their initial sexual contact. As they part on a subway car, agreeing to see each other again, the black man admits to himself that he won't be calling the other man again because he can't deal with the white man's preference for public sex.

DIRECTORY OF GAY PLAYS 73

On the Elevator by Kate Kasten. Comedy. One act. 9F. 1 interior. $10/$5.

Seven people stuck on an elevator find themselves eavesdropping on a romantic coming-out story told by one dyke to another. Claustrophobia seems to be setting in, but the seven other women also have their own stories to tell.

Once Below a Lighthouse by Ramon Delgado. Drama. One act. 2M, 1F. 1 interior. $25. Prod: The Glines, New York, 1977. Publ: in *The Best Short Plays of 1972*, Chilton Books, New York.

A shy, lonely man picks up an athletic youth near a Daytona Beach lighthouse on the strange pretext that the older man needs someone to help celebrate an anniversary. The youth, not wanting to get involved with the possible eccentricities of the older man, plays straight until the landlady exposes him as a hustler. Meanwhile, the youth has discovered the relative innocence of the older man. Stripped of their illusions, they decide to celebrate the anniversary together in each other's arms.

120 Miles Northeast of Chicago by J. Kline Hobbs. Drama. Full length. 4M, 1F. 3 exteriors.

Tully is on weekend vacation with his best friend, L.D., and Sudy, the woman L.D. is sleeping with. Tully and L.D. harass Cal, their next-door neighbor, suspecting him of being "queer," and Sudy tries to apologize for them. Lef, Cal's ex-lover, appears and gets back at Tully. Sudy befriends Cal and Lef forgives Tully. Sudy seduces Cal and Tully goes off into the dunes with Lef. All four have an awakening of themselves: Cal takes Sudy to the bus and plans to see her the next weekend; and after Tully recognizes the futility of his attachment to L.D., goes with Lef, who challenges him to a fully reciprocal relationship.

One-Liners by David Csontos. Comedy. One act. 2M. 1 exterior. $10/$5. Prod: The Glines, New York, 1977.

A skit involving two men, two phone booths, and one cruise.

One Person by Robert Patrick. Monodrama. One Act. 1M. 1 interior. $10. Prod: Old Reliable Theatre Tavern, New York, 1969. Publ: in

74   GAY THEATRE ALLIANCE

Robert Patrick's Cheep Theatricks, Samuel French, New York, 1975. Agent: Samuel French.

The author comes onstage and announces there will be no play tonight; instead he will act out his side of a love affair with a person who happens to be in the audience that night.

One Two Boy Man by Cal Yeomans. Musical. One act. (Score not available.) 2M, 1F (chorus). 1 interior.

Two men, former lovers who once traveled down very similar roads, meet after several years apart traversing highly dissimilar roads. One's journey has been completely homosexual while Two's has taken him into marriage and family life. They meet in a neutral cafe, talk, and with almost cinematic flashbacks, relive various stops in their respective trips.

Only Connect by Noel Greig and Drew Griffiths. Drama. Full length. 4M. 2 interiors. Prod: BBC, London, 1979.

Graham, 25 and a research student, visits John, 70 and retired, to interview him about Edward Carpenter. Through what he learns from John, Graham — with the help of his lover, Colin, 32 — starts to fulfill the play's title.

Oral Herstory of Lesbianism, An collaboratively written by 13 women from an idea by Terry Wolverton. Revue. 24 scenes. 13F. 1 interior (repr). Prod: Woman's Building, Los Angeles, 1979.

A collection of the true stories of the women who created it (Jerri Allyn, Nancy Angelo, Leslie Belt, Cheri Gaulke, Chutney Lu Gunderson, Brook Hallok, Sue Maberry, Louise Moore, Arlene Raven, Catherine Stifter, Cheryl Swannack, Christine Wong and Terry Wolverton), exploring issues such as coming out, coming on, mothers, racism, homophobia, incest, team sports, butch and femme roles, sexuality and lesbian future visions, combining music, dance, performance and video.

Oscar, a rhythm and blues revue based upon the life and times of Oscar Wilde by J. Camicia. Comedy/musical. One act. 6M, 5F (Doubling). Various interiors, exteriors. Prod: Hot Peaches, New York, 1978.

DIRECTORY OF GAY PLAYS 75

The events in the life of Oscar Wilde are relived in the present-day West Village by a poet/rock musician/Christopher Street Queen.

Other Side of Silence, The by Carol Pugliese. Drama. Full length. 7F (Doubling). 1 interior, 2 exteriors. $35/$15.

The play juxtaposes the housewomen, who live together, guarding their "sanity, definitions and feelings" to that of the boat women, who expose their "craziness, explorations and who explore their feelings." Threatened by both, Ana struggles between the two.

Out of the Cradle Endlessly Rocking by Eric de Lyons. Drama. Two acts. 3M, 1F. 1 interior, 1 exterior.

Jeffrey was more than a beautiful pick-up — he became the obsession of the handsome Dr. Vincent Drummond. They struggle through torment, fights and tears to close the generation gap between them and find love.

Ovens of Anita Orangejuice by Ronald Tavel. Satire. Two acts. 17M, 13F (Doubling). 6 interiors, 3 exteriors (repr). Prod: New York Theatre Strategy, New York, 1978. Agent: Helen Merrill, 337 West 22nd Street, New York, N.Y. 10011.

A documentary satire of Anita Bryant's Dade County gay rights ordinance repeal campaign and its nationwide repercussions.

P

Painted Sticks by Arthur Scott. Drama. Two acts. 5M, 3F. 5 interiors, exteriors (repr). Negotiable.

A Brechtian-like chronicling of the Negro bus boycott in Montgomery, Alabama, 1955-1956, which compares the oppression of blacks and homosexuals. The question of violent versus nonviolent resistance is raised; freedom is the issue.

Para De Noya by Fred Puliafito. Cartoon-drama. One act. 8M. 1 interior. Negotiable. Prod: Theatre Rhinoceros, San Francisco, 1978.

A gay cartoon which sets concern about gay civil liberties in a microcosm, a floating nightclub in the Sargasso Sea beseiged by the CIA. The club is run by the turbulent singer-entrepreneur, Sandrio Lupo, who lives with his boyfriend, Freydoe, who also wants to be in the show. Bascilica, Sandrio's sidekick, is formerly a drag queen from Central America who did lip-sync to American songs, but now suffers from an acute case of paranoia and fear's for Sandrio's life. Andrew, Sandrio's ex-lover, comes from Ohio to warn Sandrio about the plot, because he has first-hand government information from his job.

Passing By by Martin Sherman. Comedy-drama. Two acts. 2M. 3 interiors, 1 exterior (repr). Prod: Playwrights Horizons, New York, 1974. Agent: Charles Hunt, Fifi Oscard Associates, Inc. 19 West 44th Street, New York, N.Y. 10036.

The progress of a love affair which opens with a casual pickup in a New York cinema, is cemented over several weeks when the two men are marooned together by hepatitis, and ends when they are pulled apart by their incompatible professional ambition.

Patriot For Me, A by John Osborne. Drama. Three acts. 31M, 4F. (Extras; Doubling). 21 interiors, 2 exteriors. Prod: Royal Court Theatre, London, 1965. Publ: Faber and Faber, London, 1965. Agent: Margery Vosper Ltd., Suite 8, 26 Charing Cross Road, London WC2H 0DG, England.

In turn of the century Austria, Colonel Alfred Real has risen high in the army through hard work to overcome his humble origins. The Russian secret service has been watching his rise and assigns a female agent to seduce him, but Real is gay. He makes expensive presents to his boyfriends, and overwhelmed by debts and threats of blackmail, aids the Russians by selling them the Austrian army's secret plans. He is found out and commits suicide.

Paul and Michael by Lonnie W. Lee. Musical comedy. Two acts. (Score not available.) 10M, 5F. 1 interior. $500/$200 weekly.

One evening just after rehearsals for a show, Michael's family arrives unannounced and Paul, Michael's lover, becomes Paula, the black maid, when he is seen still in his maid costume. Paul and Michael try to hide their real relationship, Michael's father and Granny fight as always, and busy with rehearsals with the cast, Paul and Michael drop their guard and kiss in front of the family; all hell breaks loose.

Payments by Martin Bauml Duberman. Drama-comedy. Two acts. 9M, 2F (Doubling). 3 interiors. Negotiable. Prod: New Dramatists, New York, 1971. Publ: in *Male Armor: Selected Plays, 1968-1974*, E. P. Dutton, New York, 1975.

An exploration of the world of male hustling — and male closetry.

78 GAY THEATRE ALLIANCE

Pearl Divers by John Herbert. Comedy. One act. 1M, 3F. 1 interior. Negotiable. Prod: Forest Hill Chamber Theatre, Toronto, 1974. Publ: in *Some Angry Summer Songs,* Talonbooks, Vancouver, B.C., 1976. Agent: Ellen Neuwald, Inc., 905 West End Avenue, New York, N.Y. 10025.

Queenie, a flamboyant gay man, applies for a job as a waiter in a busy Toronto restaurant. The Hostess and Assistant Manager don't want to hire him because he's gay, but the woman who heads the dishwashing department meets him and wants to hire him, simply because he'll do a good job, regardless of his sexuality.

Pearls That Coalesce by Loretta Lotman. Drama. One act. 3F. Bare stage. $25/$15. Prod: Deja Vu Coffeehouse, Hollywood, 1977.

Part One of the "Carolyn Trilogy," the coming out process is seen from the inside of a single psyche. As Carolyn relives her sexual history, Carol and Lynn alternate between being her and being aspects of her hopes and her fears, her yearnings versus the societal voices. In the end, hate and fear are equally loved and understood, and are incorporated back into a single integrated personality.

People's Virgin, The by Richard Hall. Comedy. One act. 2M. 1 interior. $50/$35. Publ: in *GPU News,* Volume 7, Number 10, July 1978. Agent: Warren Bayless, Curtis Brown Ltd., 575 Madison Ave., New York, N.Y. 10022.

A mayor of New York is trying to get a gay rights bill passed, when he is interviewed by a reporter from the gay press who once had an

Perfect Relationship, A by Doric Wilson. Comedy. Two acts. 4M, 1F. 1 interior. $60/$45. Prod: The Glines, New York, 1979. Publ: in *Two Plays by Doric Wilson,* SeaHorse Press, New York, 1979. Agent: Terry Helbing, 51 West 4th Street, Room 300, New York, N.Y. 10012.

A domestic comedy, satirizing the new-found machismo prevalent in current gay male lifestyles and the resulting commitment to non-commitment. Two roommates have their relationship and apartment threatened by an opportunistic intruder. They are also visited periodically by the woman who sublet the sublet apartment to them.

DIRECTORY OF GAY PLAYS

Perfectly Normal by Robert Lynn Kazmayer. Comedy. One act. 3M, 2F. 1 interior. Negotiable.

Two teen-age men and two teen-age women who have been double-dating through high school meet one evening determined to "go all the way." They discover, however, that the strong attraction that has held the group together has been between the two men and the two women, rather than between the men and women.

Pete and Charley by John Arnold. Comedy. Two acts. 2M. Various interiors, exteriors (repr).

A weekend in New York pairs a smalltown Californian and a New Yorker. Both face the prospect of being "unfaithful" to their respective other-halves (a lover and a wife) when they find themselves falling in love.

Pink Satin Bombers Present an Evening of Faggot Theatre by The Pink Satin Bombers Collective. Revue. Three acts. 6M (Doubling). 1 interior (repr). Negotiable. Prod: DeWitt Mall, Ithaca, New York, 1977. Agent: Calamus Books, P.O. Box 689, Cooper Station, New York, N.Y. 10003.

Selections from gay history form a prelude to Part One: Getting Ready to Go Out; The Bar (dance piece); The Morning After; Gossiping on the Phone. Part Two: Twelve short scenes depicting significant moments in the development as individuals which everyone has experienced, followed by six scenes (one for each member of the company) about coming out to one's parents. Part Three: A one-act play in five scenes about a teacher accidentally forced to come out and faced with the decision to fight for his job despite difficulties for his students and loved ones.

Play by Shelly Zaikis. Drama with music. One act. (Laura Nyro's albums or music used.) 5M, 2F (Doubling). 1 interior.

Billie has had a relationship with another woman, Jo, and is now in conflict and fighting a relationship — mainly in her head — with a man, Johnny Joe. The script also concerns consciousness and loyalty in love realms, and lends itself to dance (interwoven with lyrics) and flashbacks.

Play House by Joseph Gath. Drama. Three acts. 2M, 1F. 1 interior. Prod: Mercer Arts Center, New York, 1972.

In the late 1950's Steve and Joel are lovers, and Steve is surprised to meet Mary Jane, Joel's wife, whom he married to be able to stay in the U.S. and has not seen for five years. Mary Jane is funny-looking and a lot of fun, a "fag-hag" type and wins Steve over and announces that she is pregnant. Steve enjoys doing her over, but Joel is upset and asks her to leave; Mary Jane threatens to have him deported. Joel shows her his citizenship papers and tells her to leave; she does, planning to go to another gay couple she knows.

Pogey Bait by George Birimisa. Drama. Two acts. 6M (Doubling). 2 interiors. $25/$20. Prod: Las Palmas Theatre, Hollywood, 1977. Publ: in *Drummer* magazine, numbers 12 and 13, San Francisco, 1977.

Joey Jurovich goes to the Captain of his destroyer during the Second World War and tells him that he is gay. The Captain tries to get Joey to admit that he has been making it with Lefty Lefko, the Chief Petty Officer, whom the Captain hates.

Point Charges by Eric Allyn. Drama. Two acts. 6M, 2F. 3 interiors.

Tom Wilk, a 20-year-old student, nervously anticipates coming out to his parents at a Wilk Family pre-reunion-get-together, hosted by his cousin Phil, a 38-year-old electrical engineer, and his lover, Marc, a 34-year-old pediatrician. Tom is inspired by their ten-year relationship, but doesn't know about Marc's furtive visits to the baths and Phil's hostility. Tom rejoins his boyfriend, Bobby, 20, whose ideas about love and lovers broke up their relationship. Tom's and Phil's parents arrive, to further complicate matters, as scenes occur between the various men and parents.

Points of Departure by Paul Stephen Lim. Drama. One act. 2M, 2F. 1 interior. Negotiable. Prod: East West Players, Los Angeles, 1977. Agent: Biff Liff, William Morris Agency, 1350 Avenue of the Americas, New York, N.Y. 10019.

A young writer in the Philippines dreams of life in the United States, and his married life is complicated when an American publisher offers him all the necessary immigration papers — but with strings attached.

Poiret in Exile by Cal Yeomans. Drama. One act. 1M. 1 interior. Prod: Alma Rainbow Productions, San Francisco, 1979.

A monologue for a grand old man currently living the life of a casualty in the Tenderloin in San Francisco. He talks of the way it was and looks forward to an incomprehensible tomorrow.

Posturings by John Arnold. Drama. Two acts. 7M, 1F. 2 interiors. Prod: American Conservatory Theatre, San Francisco, 1977.

In pre-World War II Berlin, a man is forced to choose between his younger lover and what he believes to be his only chance for survival. The play is primarily about choices, especially the choice to take a stand for one's beliefs.

Prayer for My Daughter, A by Thomas Babe. Drama. Full length. 4M. 1 interior. Prod: New York Shakespeare Festival Public Theatre, New York, 1978.

An elderly woman has been murdered for a small amount of money and the two suspects are a neurotic middle-aged homosexual and his young junkie friend. They are questioned by two policemen: one a large caricatured tough guy, the other smaller and more sympathetic; the first is a drunk, the second is on drugs. The homosexual considers his friend his "daughter," and has an actual daughter of his own, as does the tough policeman, whose daughter commits suicide during the course of the play.

Prisoner of Love by Richard Hall. Comedy. One act. 3M. 1 interior, 1 exterior. $50/$35. Prod: The Glines, New York, 1978. Agent: Warren Bayless, Curtis Brown Ltd., 575 Madison Avenue, New York, N.Y. 10022.

A gay liberationist visits Puerto Rico, where a wealthy friend treats him to the services of a hustler without telling him about it. Complications ensue when he finds himself falling in love with the hustler.

Private Passions by Fredric Stephan. Comedy. Two acts. 7M, 3F. 1 exterior.

A young man's mother marries his ex-lover and various events happen as a result.

P.S. Your Cat Is Dead! by James Kirkwood. Comedy-drama. Two acts. 3M, 1F. 1 interior. Prod: Golden Theatre, New York, 1975. Publ: Samuel French, New York, 1979. Agent: Esther Sherman, William Morris Agency, 1350 Avenue of the Americas, New York, N.Y. 10019.

On New Year's Eve, James Zoole, 38, gets fired from a play, written out of a soap opera, his cat is sick with a kidney infection and he comes home to find his girl friend packing up to leave him. On top of this he catches Vito, a burglar, about to rip him off for the third time. He succeeds in knocking him out and ties him to the kitchen sink, venting all the anger he feels about his profession and life upon him. To his surprise, he finds he has not only a bisexual burglar tied up, but he is also a human being, and the two form a bizarre friendship of sorts.

Quadrille by Gregory Peterson. Romantic comedy. Three acts. 3M, 1F. 2 interiors. Negotiable. Prod: Equity Library Theatre, New York, 1979.

Vincent, a young manager of opera singers, and Valerie, his outrageous woman friend, both pursue wild notions of romance with Ross and Jean-Pierre, whom they believe will fulfill their passionate desires. A complicated love quadrangle develops when it is learned that Ross and Jean-Pierre are already proclaimed to be lovers. As both have liaisons with the men, they discover the value of the love and friendship they have for each other.

Queen's Will, The by Wallace Hamilton. Comedy. Two acts. 11M, 1F (Doubling). 1 interior. Prod: Dramatis Personae, New York, 1978. Agent: Robert Freedman, Brandt and Brandt, 1501 Broadway, New York, N.Y. 10036.

A story of what happened to five drag queens who participated in the Stonewall Riots of 1969. Before her death after the riots, Sheila, one of the queens, left a will forecasting what would happen to her sisters. One by one her prophecies come true, and only the last is unfulfilled — that Ginger would die before her 28th birthday. The play opens on the eve of that birthday, with Ginger terror-stricken. The plot is revealed in multiple flashbacks, including some of the riot itself. Ginger manages to survive.

R

Rags by Philip Real. Drama. Two acts. 13M, 4F (Doubling). 2 interiors. Negotiable. Prod: Theatre Rhinoceros, San Francisco, 1978.

Matt works in a clothing shop in Chicago and spends most of his nights at discos. Patrick, a co-worker, resents Matt, feeling he's decadent, and harasses him. Matt is angry with the macho attitudes in the store, but doesn't confront them. He meets Larry at a disco and has an affair, ending with Larry making Matt see that he doesn't want a long-term relationship. Matt and Patrick finally have a showdown, and ultimately Matt realizes, with the help of Larry and others, that he can overcome his ambivalence and confusion and stand up to Patrick and the rest of the straight world.

Rainbow in the Night, A by George Birimisa. Drama. Full length. 2M, 3F. 2 interiors (unit). $25/$20. Prod: Matrix Theatre Group, Hollywood, 1978.

Joey is gay but falls in love with Dinah; it is a tough realization for him that he is gay — the play takes place in the 1950's.

Recorder, The by Martin Bauml Duberman. Drama-comedy. One act. 2M. 1 interior. Negotiable. Prod: Tambellini's Gate Theatre, New York, 1970. Publ: in *The Best Short Plays of 1970,* Chilton Books, New York, 1970.

DIRECTORY OF GAY PLAYS 85

An interview between a young historian and a legendary, never-identified older man. The play operates on various levels of role shifts and sexual innuendo, centering on the theme of "memory," personal and historical.

Red by Mark Dunster. Comedy. Two acts. 8M. 1 interior, 1 exterior. Publ: Linden Publishers, New York, 1979.

Eight males and their interrelated sexual and other relationships, set in a New York garden apartment.

Red Star by C. D. Arnold. Drama. One act. 2M, 1F. 1 interior. $15/$10. Prod: Earnest Players, San Francisco, 1979.

Ernest brings home Harry, his very first man from the Red Star Saloon, and through the course of the evening, he awakens to the joys of opening himself to strangers. Enter Sally Bananas, a free-wheeling dragon whose sole purpose is to deliver "Ernie" from the horrors of fly-by-night encounters, turning the evening into a blatant tug-of-war.

Rents by Michael Wilcox. Comedy-drama. Full length. 5M. Prod: Traverse Theatre Club, Edinburgh, Scotland, 1979.

Newcastle lecturer Richard Ridley goes to Charles Stuart College, Edinburgh, for a few weeks of relief lecturing and becomes absorbed in the life of Phil MacPherson, a drama student there, and becomes involved in the gay life of the city.

Reverie's Telecast by David Emerson Smith. Political drama. One act. 9M (Doubling). 1 exterior. $15/$10. Prod: Theatre Rhinoceros, San Francisco, 1978. Publ: in *Fag Rag,* Spring-Summer, 1979.

In twelve scenes, the play alternates between street scenes and telepathic communications between two Mexican lovers: Carlos in Mexico and Jesus hustling on Polk Street. The street scenes are based on the author's personal experiences of events that took place in September 1977. A TV station did an expose about young gay hustlers on Polk Street, and alarmed business people had police arrest almost anyone standing in front of a business — a new city ordinance. Street people and hustlers organized and picketed.

Richmond Jim by Cal Yeomans. Drama. One act. 3M. 1 interior. Prod: Theatre Rhinoceros, San Francisco, 1979.

A young boy from Virginia goes home with his first trick while visiting the Big Apple and finds himself deeply immersed in the world of S & M and leather sex.

Rights, The by George Whitmore. Comedy-drama. Two acts. 3M, 1F. 1 exterior. Prod: The Glines, New York, 1980.

Larry, a failed writer, is invited to Fire Island to sign the rights away on a play he wrote with Paul when they were lovers in the 1950's, but Larry refuses to play. Only after he digs into the past with Paul does Larry make up his mind. Paul's lover, Buddy, helps him to do so.

Ritz, The by Terrence McNally. Comedy. Full length. 14M, 3F. Various interiors. $50/$35. Prod: (as *The Tubs*), Yale Rep, New Haven, Connecticut, 1973. Longacre Theatre, New York, 1975. Publ: Dodd, Mead, New York, 1976. Agent: Samuel French.

Proclo, chubby, straight, square and middle-aged, is running from the Mafia and decides to hide out in the safest place, a gay bath. A chubby chaser goes after him, as do some Mafia types, who in turn are being chased by a handsome, falsetto-voiced detective. Also there is a Puerto Rican bathhouse singer who dreams of making it Bette Midler-style who wants to find someone to be her producer.

Ruffian on the Stair, The by Joe Orton. Drama. One act. 2M, 1F. 1 interior. $20/$15. Prod: Royal Court Theatre, London, 1967. Publ: in *Complete Plays of Joe Orton,* Grove Press, New York, 1977. Agent: Margaret Ramsay Limited, 14A Goodwin's Court, St. Martins Lane, London WC2N, 4L1, England.

At the home of a laborer and a woman he lives with, a stranger appears one day asking for a room; he begins taunting her and almost resorts to viciousness. He returns the next day and the laborer is there; he has killed by hit-and-run the homosexual lover and brother of the stranger. The stranger pretends to ravish the woman, forcing the laborer to shoot him.

S

Satyricon by Paul Foster. Black comedy. Two acts. 9M, 7F (+ chorus). 1 interior. $35/$25. Prod: LaMama E.T.C., New York, 1972. Publ: in *The Off-Off Broadway Book,* Bobbs-Merrill, Indianapolis, Indiana, 1972. Agent: Samuel French.

Based on Petronius' first-century novella, Petronius, Nero's Master of the Revels, must invent diversions for the crazed tyrant. Petronius uses three young lovers; his efforts to arbitrate their feuds, while controlling Nero's homicidal impulses, are too much for him. The lovers run away when Nero decides to kill Petronius and set fire to the city. Petronius commits suicide as the city burns.

Save It For Your Death Bed by Randolph Carter. Black comedy. One act. 3M, 1F. 1 interior. Negotiable. Prod: Cherry Lane Theatre, New York, 1968.

Geraldine, a young and beautiful drag queen, escapes from a club where she is the star performer with George, who is very square, but madly in love with her, in order to escape Nick, a small-time gangster. George's mother is upset by the "floozy" he brings to their house in Queens. Nick shows up, Geraldine kills him, and he is buried under the floor in the living room. As George's mother helps

Geraldine fit into her wedding dress, she discovers her true identity, and is gratified her son is not involved with another woman, and possibly knew of the deceit all along.

Scrap of Paper by James Purdy. Drama. One act. 2F. 1 interior. Prod: Ensemble Studio Theatre, New York, 1978.

The play concerns the deep emotional dependence between two women, Mrs. Bankers and her black maid, Naomi Greene.

Season in the Sun by Wolcott Gibbs. Comedy. Three acts. 9M, 6F. 1 exterior. Prod: Cort Theatre, New York, 1950. Publ: Random House, New York, 1951.

On Fire Island a magazine writer is staying at a guest house trying to write a book, and having great difficulty doing so. Also at the house are two outrageous gay male guests. Eventually, the writer returns to his magazine job.

Sex Machine, The by Robert Lynn Kazmayer. Drama. One act. 1M, 1F. 1 interior. Negotiable.

A multi-media theatre piece in which two burlesque dancers describe their lives as they go through their dance numbers. In the background, slides are projected showing scenes from their lives and their environment. As the piece progresses, it becomes evident that they are both trapped in their views of themselves as sexual objects.

Sex Show: Comedy Madness by Daniel Curzon. Satire. Two acts. 6M or F (any combination). Bare stage. Negotiable. Prod: Gay Community Center, San Francisco, 1977.

Sixteen satirical skits about sex — from bestiality to cruising in a gay bar. The actors act, mime and play multiple roles — from an All-American family watching a Walt Disney porn movie to a little child being fought over by his divorced parents.

Sextet by Harvey Perr and Lee Goldsmith. Musical. One act. (Score available.) 4M, 2F. 1 interior. Prod: Bijou Theatre, New York, 1974. Agent: Flora Roberts, 65 East 55th Street, Suite 702, New York, N.Y. 10022.

Saturday night in New York City at the apartment of two gay male lovers; one of them has invited his old college chum to dinner and his mother has invited herself. The college chum brings his wife; the mother brings her new boyfriend. Lots of feelings — old and new — arise, and each character discovers something about him/herself and his/her relationship. A kind of battle of the sexes and the generations ensues.

Shadow Box, The by Michael Cristofer. Drama. Two acts. 5M, 5F. 4 interiors. $50/$35. Prod: Mark Taper Forum, Los Angeles, 1975. Publ: Avon Books, New York, 1978. Agent: Samuel French.

A study of the contemplation of death by three terminally ill patients and their families. One of the three, Brian, is being cared for by his lover, Mark, and the two are visited by Brian's former wife, Beverly, who has not previously met Mark.

She's Like Vanilla, My Hudmilla by C. C. Fish. Musical-drama-comedy. Three acts. (Sheet music available.) 5M, 8F (Doubling). 1 interior, 1 exterior.

The play alternates between a dark alley and a lively cafe during the winter of 1979 in San Francisco. In the alley, Charley Moonsilver, a lesbian playwright, speaks and sings to her spirits and encounters the mysteries and fears of a woman alone in a dark male-hostile environment. In the cafe, the sexual and romantic struggles and motivations of seven gay men and women develop, with the various roles and relationships they adopt. In an interlude after the second act, "Our Shades Lifted Slightly," five spirits of symbolic yet personal natures debate the destiny of Charley.

Ships by Alan Wakeman. Drama. Three acts. 6M, 1F. 1 interior, 2 exteriors. Prod: Inter-Action's Almost Free Theatre (Gay Sweatshop), London, 1975. Publ: in *Homosexual Acts,* Ambiance/Almost Free Playscripts, London, 1975. Agent: Spokesmen, 1 Craven Hill, London W2 3EW, England.

Three linked one-act plays: "Coffee" — a man is attracted to the repairman who comes to fix a gas leak; the scene is performed twice: once as it happens and again with each character's subtext added. "Tea" — the same man finds a woman sobbing in the subway and charitably invites her home for a cup of tea. "Wine" — a gay freak meets three scruffy men in a park and shares his wine with them; they talk about gay love and the "honest souls who are the children of the future age."

Shroud by Douglas Derek Roome. Drama. One act. 2M, 1F. 1 exterior. Negotiable.

Three people meet at the site of a geomagnetic anomaly on the Northern California coast: a young fantasy writer (male and heterosexual) searching for inspiration; a high school student (female and bi) intent upon a science project; and a young alien (incarnated in male human form) seeking a portal back to his/her monosexual people. The play examines identity, self-perception and androgyny.

Sinking Sinking by David Csontos and Kathy Burke Hill. Musical farce. Two acts. (Tape and sheet music available.) 7M, 12F Doubling). 4 interiors, 1 exterior. $50/$35. Prod: Illick's Mill Theatre, Bethlehem, PA, 1976.

Fun, frolic and filth on board the Titanic.

Sirens, The by Wes Muchmore. Farce. One act. 1M, 3F (or drags). 1 exterior. Prod: (in Spanish) Compania Teatral-Huatusco, Veracruz, Mexico, 1978.

The three sirens, on their Mediterranean isle, tire of luring men to their doom so they revolt, only to learn that revolution takes some forethought, as well as passionate feeling.

Sissy by Seth Allen. Musical Comedy. One act. (Tape and sheet music available.) 15M, 6F ,Doubling). 1 exterior. $50/$10. Prod: LaMama E.T.C., New York, 1973.

A group of people in front of the Paramount Mountain look for love, money and power.

DIRECTORY OF GAY PLAYS   91

'67 by Robert Wallace. Drama with music. Two acts. (Supremes records used for music.) 7M, 4F (Doubling). 1 interior (repr). Agent: Great North Agency Limited, 345 Adelaide Street West, Toronto, Ontario M5V 1R5.

   A successful university professor and master manipulator faces "a new generation with new expectations" and a tempestuous relationship with a new student in the fall of 1967.

Sluts by Ross MacLean. Farce. Two acts. 7M, 2F. 1 exterior. Negotiable. Prod: Deja Vu Coffeehouse, Hollywood, 1979.

   In a group of free-wheeling young men, one of the members accidentally becomes a Christian during a bad drug deal. He in turn converts his companions to the good life, undermining the social structure of the group, and perpetrating a string of criminal events to land non-believers in jail. All their lives are permanently damaged as a result, though they exalt in being good men of the Lord.

Sodom, or the Quintessence of Debauchery by John Wilmot, Earl of Rochester. Satire. Five acts. 9M, 6F (extras). 1 interior. Publ: Brandon House, North Hollywood, CA, 1966.

   A satire of King Charles II and his court, about a king who decrees that "buggery" is to replace conventional sex; the play includes scenes on masturbation, anal intercourse, sex during menstruation, bestiality, sex with dildos, etc. (Written in 1660 and actually performed for the King's court.)

Soft Core Kid, The by Frank Hogan and Walter Kubran. Farce. Two acts. 8M, 2F. 1 interior. $50/$35. Prod: The Glines, New York, 1976. Agent: Terry Helbing, 51 West 4th Street, Room 300, New York 10012.

   A mother decides to settle her 16-year-old son's life for him, when she discovers he is frittering away his youth with not one — but three — older and very eligible male admirers. Sorting out those who play-and-run-away from those who stay-love-and-care, mama finds husbands for both her son and herself while liberating new fonts of sexual freedom. The play takes place in a multi-doored photographer's studio and uses photographic projections.

Somebody's Angel Child by Cal Yeomans. Drama. One act. 1M. 1 interior.

A monologue for a transvestite en route transsexual living in a Tenderloin hotel in San Francisco. An image play, written to be illuminated with a slide show behind the words.

Song At Twilight, A by Noel Coward. Comedy. Full length. 2M, 2F. 1 interior. $50/$25. Prod: Queen's Theatre, London, 1966. Publ: Heinemann Books, London, 1966. Agent: Samuel French.

A cosmopolite author in his later years is caught between two women: one, his wife of convenience of twenty years; the other, one of his former loves. The latter has some love letters that she is about to turn over to a biographer, but he objects, because it would hurt his reputation. She produces another set of love letters, written to a male friend of his early youth. The wife of convenience says that she knew this all along, and sends off the former flame, her blackmail plan failed.

Splitting Image by Colin Spencer. Comedy. One act. 7M, 7F (Doubling). Prod: London, 1968. Publ: in *Plays and Players,* London, September, 1968.

One half of a gay male couple discovers that he is pregnant. Various people try to convince him not to have the child, but he does so anyway. The FBI gets involved, only to discover that numerous gay men are in a similar situation.

Split Lips by Ralph Carideo. Comedy. Three acts. 4M, 2F. 1 interior. Negotiable.

Half of a gay male couple and the female half of a straight couple enter into an intimate relationship, much to the annoyance of their lovers who are thus brought together and forced to confront one another. The scene is two neighboring apartments, both visible at the same time. The two characters who are having the relationship are split into two personalities — portrayed by four actors — and there is much simultaneous and overlapping dialogue. Everyone's feelings get entangled, forcing a reassessment of relationships. The gay couple survives through sheer stamina.

Sport of Men and Boys, The by Ross H. Jones. Drama. One act. 9M. 1 interior.

Over several games of pool in a gay bar, nine gay men discuss being gay: how each discovered he was gay, his childhood crushes, how he came out, and responses to religion and loneliness. One of them, a leather man, continually calls the others faggots and eventually has a fight with the drag queen. The leather man reveals his pain over losing a childhood buddy and he and the drag queen resolve their differences.

Squirrel Loves You by Ralph Carideo. Drama. Two acts. 3M, 1 interior. Negotiable.

Two roommates fall in love without realizing it. It isn't until one tries to take away the other's lover that this realization occurs to each in separate, lonely moments. Through their dealings with this third person they are able to confront their fear of love and overcome it. The last scene has one waiting for the return of the other and the beginning of a new life.

Staircase by Charles Dyer. Drama. Full length. 2M. 1 interior. $50/$25. Prod: Royal Shakespeare Company, Aldwych, England, 1966. Publ: Grove Press, New York, 1966. Agent: Samuel French.

Two seedy old barbers ("hair stylists") on their day off, Sunday, give each other trims, manicures and what only they can give each other, love. One is a motherly old boy, and the other a middle-aged juvenile actor; both are failures. The younger man has been caught in a transvestite situation and is due before the magistrate. The other once fathered a daughter, and is awaiting her first visit in twenty years.

Steambath by Bruce Jay Friedman. Morality drama. Full length. 12M, 2F. 1 interior. $50/$25. Prod: Truck and Warehouse Theatre, New York, 1970. Publ: Alfred A. Knopf, New York, 1971. Agent: Samuel French.

Set in a steambath, a girl walks into a men's area, takes a public shower and then retires, leaving the stage to two homosexuals who do a song and dance in lip sync. A Puerto Rican enters who gives orders to a scanning TV monitor and causes various events to happen; a new arrival does not believe he has so much god-like power.

Steve and Angelo by Barry Frauman. Drama. One act. 3M. 1 interior.

Angelo Rossi, editor of the *Lambda Herald,* has just returned from L.A. and Steve Efrem, with whom he has been having a relationship, comes over for a date. They are interrupted by business calls because of needed coverage on an upcoming rally protest against homophobic legislation. Steve is upset that Angelo is a workaholic and never seems to have enough time for their relationship. As Steve is about to leave, his friend Michael arrives, having just broken up with his lover. Angelo hears from his mother in New York, who has just thrown his father out for having an affair, and Angelo tries to mediate. When Steve returns to try to comfort him and suggests that they live together, Angelo refuses, because of his background and current activities, since he cannot return Steve's feelings.

Strange Bedfellows by Mark McHenry. Comedy. Full length.

The bedtime behavior of two gay men whose lovemaking is constantly being interrupted by people from their past.

Stranger At the Window by Richard Erickson and Dean McIlnay. Comedy-drama. Two acts. 3M, 5F. 1 interior. 5%/gross.

A young writer is battling alcoholism while trying to write his first novel at a Cape Cod cottage haunted by the ghost of a beautiful girl, which the realtor (a gay ex-WAC sergeant) keeps quiet about. A fag-hag next-door neighbor tells him about it, but he has already seen her walking on the patio. The neighbor introduces him to a gay man, and after he tries to make him, the two become friends. The writer sees the ghost again, beckoning to him, and the two leap off the patio to the ocean below. Prospective new renters see the couple outside the window, but the realtor refuses to admit it.

Strangers and Other Lovers by Harry H. Long and Joseph Uher. Drama. Full length. 2M. 1 interior.

A reflection of the reaching out to touch someone else, as two men grow from high school pals and lovers into adults shaped by time; various twists, turns and comic bends separate the men, and random shifts bring them together again.

DIRECTORY OF GAY PLAYS 95

Streamers by David Rabe. Drama. Full length. 11M. 1 interior. $50/$35. Prod: Long Wharf Theatre, New Haven, Connecticut, 1976. Publ: Alfred A. Knopf, New York, 1977. Agent: Samuel French.

In an army barracks room are three very different soldiers: a young intellectual, a street-smart black and a homosexual. The latter has a crush on the first, who refuses his advances; to try to win his affections, he flirts with Carlyle, a dangerous psychopathic black from the ghetto, who eventually murders the intellectual and an older sergeant.

Street Theatre by Doric Wilson. Comedy. One act. 12M, 2F. 1 exterior. $40/$35. Agent: Terry Helbing, 51 West 4th Street, Room 300, New York, N.Y. 10012.

A political satire: Christopher Street people the hour preceding the Stonewall Riots in 1969; their attitudes, role differences and conflicts. Companion piece to ***The Ad Hoc Committee*** (q.v.).

Support Circle, The by Barry Stewart. Drama. One act. 7M. 1 interior.

A fifteen-minute dramatization of a gay men's "coming out" group. There is little action or interaction between the characters, as much of the script consists of monologues.

Swamp Play #2: The Earthly Chariot by Cal Yeomans. Drama. One act. 14M, 2F (Doubling). Multiple interiors, exteriors.

The story of a young boy in the old south who comes to believe that "the Lord got mixed-up" and put a woman's soul in his body. When this gender confusion causes him to be ejected from home, he begins to pass as a woman and comes to believe he is one as he searches zealously for God in a world that has no place for transvestite religiosity.

Sweaters and Monogamy by Y. Harrington. Comedy-drama. Two acts. 4M, 2F. 1 interior. $50/$35. Agent: Terry Helbing, 51 West 4th Street, Room 300, New York, N.Y. 10012.

An examination of gay men who tire of backroom bars, baths, piers, trucks — that is, quick sex — and who go beyond that to try to find new ways to relate to each other. The play also examines an intimate, but nonsexual relationship between a gay man and a straight woman (but who is not a "fag-hag") who share an apartment.

T

Taste of Honey, A by Shelagh Delaney. Drama. Two acts. 3M, 2F. 1 interior. Prod: Theatre Royal, London, 1958. Publ: Grove Press, New York, 1959. Agent: CMA, 99 Park Lane, London W1, England.

Jo, a young girl, follows the promiscuous behavior of her mother, Helen, but maintains the innocence of a sensitive child. She plans to leave but is jealous of her mother's playboy fiance and has an affair with a black sailor. When he goes overseas, she finds a job and a friend with Geoffrey, a gay man. He is attentive to her when she is pregnant, but the mother returns and drives him away.

Tea and Sympathy by Robert Anderson. Drama. Full length. 9M, 2F. 1 interior. $50/$25. Prod: Ethel Barrymore Theatre, New York, 1953. Publ: Random House, New York, 1953. Agent: Samuel French.

A boy at a boarding school is teased by his classmates because he has played women's roles in amateur theatricals and because he is very sensitive. The teasing turns to rumor and then persecution. The master of the house he is staying in joins in the persecution, and the boy's father doesn't understand him. Determined to prove his manliness, the boy goes out for a night with the town "strumpet," sickens at the sight of her, and runs home. He is now shunned, and the master's wife offers him the only sympathy he can find.

GAY THEATRE ALLIANCE

Thanksgiving Lesbian, A by Loretta Lotman. Drama. Two acts. 2M, 6F. 1 interior. Negotiable.

The second play in the "Carolyn" trilogy, Carolyn Mannings, fully integrated and self-accepting since **Pearls That Coalesce** (q.v.), returns home to her family's Thanksgiving celebration for the first time since coming out to each of them individually. The family is ruled by Carolyn's widowed mother, Laina, in her fifties, a businesswoman who compulsively prepares a ritual Thanksgiving, while exerting controls over other family members.

There You Are by Graham Jackson. Comedy. One act. 1M, 2F. 1 interior. $25/$10. Prod: UC Playhouse, Toronto, 1979.

Attending the funeral of a mutual "friend's" mother, two female representatives of the new rich find themselves embroiled in a discussion about the homosexuality of two young men of their acquaintance — much to the chagrin of the man sitting next to them.

They Do It With Mirrors by R. Dale Wilson. Drama-comedy. One act. 2M. 1 interior. $35/$25.

The bedroom only story of a love affair, chronicling the moments of private despair as two men try to form love to their own expectations and in the process miss the real thing in its own form. This play examines the nature of possession as it is confused with love.

Thinking Straight by Laurence Collinson. Drama. One act. 2M. 1 interior. Prod: Inter-Action's Almost Free Theatre (Gay Sweatshop), London, 1975. Publ: in *Homosexual Acts*, Ambiance/Almost Free Playscripts, London, 1975. Agent: Margery Vosper Ltd., Suite 8, 26 Charing Cross Road, London WC2H, 0DG, England.

Ten years after he has written a TV play, the playwright discusses the merits of the script with the female character he wrote in the play then and the gay male character (a younger version of himself) whom the female was meant to be.

Third Person by Andrew Rosenthal. Drama. Two acts. 3M, 3F. 1 interior. Prod: Arts Theatre Club, London, 1951. Publ: in *Plays of the Year,* Volume 7, Elek Books Ltd., London, 1953. Agent: MCA Ltd., 35 Dover Street, London W1, England.

Kip Ames, who is both sinister and charming, has returned to Hank Moilland's home in New York City after World War II, in which the two served together. The other members of the household, including Hank's wife, feel that Kip has been staying too long, and aware of their relationship, have Hank force Kip to leave.

To the Tune of a Military Drummer by Lonnie W. Lee. Comedy-drama. Two acts. 11M. 1 interior. $750/$250 (weekly).

A group of ten young men, 18-20 years of age, are brought together at a military school. All are strangers with a few problems. Roger Fairchild and Sam Wagner become fast and close friends. Roger finds his rough military Company Commander attractive, while Sam finds Hightower attractive, not knowing of his pill habit and the fact that he is 25 years old passing for 20. Jack Lovelace, the Company Leader, always trying to be impressive with his military manner and his macho appearance, also has a secret. Larry O'Connors has a pill problem until he ends up hanged. Roger and Jack have a few words, and the next day, Jack is found with much blood on his bed and the back of his skull cracked.

Toilet, The by LeRoi Jones (Imamu Amiri Baraka). Drama. One act. 11M. 1 interior. Prod: St. Mark's Playhouse, New York, 1964. Publ: Grove Press, New York, 1967. Agent: Claire S. Degener, 75 East 55th Street, New York, N.Y. 10022.

Set in a public toilet, a play about love between a white and a black boy, which, because of the brutality of the social order, cannot find expression.

Tom and Jerry by Ross H. Jones. Drama. Two acts. 4M (Doubling). 1 interior. Negotiable.

Jerry and Allen trick and then later, Tom and Jerry talk about Allen, about Tom's ex-wife and about Jerry's confused and wandering existence. Tom offers to help Jerry out by staying in his house while he is in New York for ten days. After flashbacks, Jerry remembers that how he met Tom is just like how he met Allen. Tom returns and asks Jerry to leave; Jerry doesn't understand and breaks down, and Jerry's developing madness is seen in flashbacks. Jerry leaves and Tom is shot in the chest (a real or psychological wound?). Jerry and David then trick, a duplication of all Jerry's tricking.

Too Much Man by Ralph Carideo. Comedy. Three acts. 3M, 1F. 2 interiors. Negotiable.

A woman returns to rekindle an old relationship with a younger man only to find that he is much better off now that he is gay and living with another man. However, he is not getting along with his lover because of the threat of the past relationship with the woman; he would like to go off with her. Seeing him now, she no longer wants him, nor does his current lover, who wants a more stable relationship. When he moves in with a rich dilettante, both decide he must be rescued and returned, though it is not resolved to whom. In the end, the woman brings him back and the man holds him.

Total Eclipse by Christopher Hampton. Drama. Full length. 10M, 5F (+ extras). Various interiors, exteriors. $50/$25. Prod: Royal Court Theatre, London 1968. Publ: Faber and Faber, London, 1969. Agent: Samuel French.

The relationship between poets Rimbaud and Verlaine and an examination of the bourgeois and artistic societies of the period. The contrast between the two men is developed, as well as their mutual need for each other as they move through and away from the literary life of the time and from Verlaine's wife and her family. The poets are shown in their private timeless world that they built together and ends on a note of violence to show how fragile it was.

Train to Babylon, The by Robert Esposito. Drama. One act. 2F. 1 interior. Prod: Triad Playwrights.

Two suburban housewives have at each other in more ways than one while their husbands and sons attend a hockey game in the city.

Trans-Lesblanic Follies by Loretta Lotman. Political satire. One act. 14F (Doubling). Minimal set. $25/$10. Prod: Gay Academic Union Conference, New York, 1975.

An eight-sketch revue satirizing the lesbian-feminist movement, based on the contradiction between rhetoric and human foible. Sketches include: "The Conference," "The Great Invisible Lesbian," "Bartalk," "The Art Show I and II," "Ms. Lesbiettiquette," "Woman Alone at a Bar," and "Support."

Trevor by John Bowen. Comedy. One act. 4M, 4F. 1 interior. Prod: Hampstead Theatre Club, London, 1968. Publ and Agent: Samuel French (London).

Two gay women live together and have each invented a fiance, Trevor, to tell their parents about. When one set of parents is due to visit, one of the women goes to a bar and picks up a man whom they pay to impersonate the fiance. The other set of parents also arrives unexpectedly, and eventually the women tell their parents the truth, but they refuse to acknowledge it.

Trick by J. Neil Harris. Drama. One act. 2M. 1 interior.

Tom and Andy have "morning-after" small-talk conversation after having tricked the night before. The scene is repeated, and this time each expresses his thoughts (to himself) of what he would really like to say. Both would like the relationship to go beyond this morning, but neither can find a way to express himself.

Trophy, The by Joel Ensana. Drama. One act. 2M, 1F. 1 interior. Negotiable.

A psychological drama, looking into what happens when a man locks his "feminine" self within his "masculine" self; a tragic comedy-of-errors dealing with the theme of repression.

True by James Purdy. Drama. One act. 2M. 1 interior. Prod: Westbeth Theatre Center, New York, 1978. Publ: in *Two Plays by James Purdy*, New London Press, Dallas, TX, 1979. Agent: Gilbert Parker, Curtis Brown Ltd., 575 Madison Avenue, New York, N.Y. 10022.

Concerns two young brothers, the older of whom has murdered a man who ridiculed his almost obsessive caring for his younger brother; the younger boy has accidentally seen his brother commit the murder, but in a state of shock, cannot credit what he sees. The play centers on the two brothers' struggle to admit the painful truths of their lives, and the final revelation results in the death of both boys.

T-Shirts by Robert Patrick. Comedy. One act. 3M. 1 interior. Prod: Out and About Theatre, Minneapolis, 1978. Publ: in *Gay Plays,* Avon Books, New York, 1979.

Marvin, 40, famed playwright, and Kink, 30, rising interior decorator, are confronted with Tom, 20, taking shelter from the rain.

Tubstrip by A. J. Kronengold. Comedy. Two acts. 9M. 1 interior. Prod: Mercer Arts Center, New York, 1973.

One weekday evening at a popular New York City gay bath house. Nine men, representing a full cross-section of all gay types, cross paths during the evening at the baths.

Tug-of-War by John A. Dentinger, Jr. Drama. Two acts. 4M, 1F. 2 interiors.

Mark Stockton and Don Wheeler are two young roommates who could be lovers except that their cynical world views prevent them from expressing any affection for each other. When Don announces his decision to move out, Mark seeks a roommate in Brian Davis, an older would-be lover who may or may not be gay. Mark finds he can express his feelings with Brian and tries to help Brian face his sexual identity. Don returns to find him spending the night. Andrea Harris, their friend, helps them realize that the people they've invested so much emotion in are frauds. Both are crushed, but Mark recovers enough to make an overture to Don, who is now too numb to accept what he longed for all along. He moves out, taking with him the last of Mark's discarded romantic illusions.

Tug of War by Alan Rossett. Melodrama. Two acts. 3M, 3F. Unit set. Negotiable. Prod: Roundabout Theatre, New York, 1971.

"You were broke, you needed a bath, Mopsy came along." Thus she explains their relationship to Peter, her kept young homosexual, lest he get sentimental. She has other things in mind, like throwing him into the arms of someone she's decided to destroy: Lilane, aging, mysterious, already on the brink of insanity. A game for power ensues, playing on the fears and fantasies of childhood.

Two and Two Are One by Kenneth Harris. Drama. Full length. 6M. 1 exterior. Negotiable.

A modern Greek drama based on the Narcissus legend and the conflict of religious concepts of Apollo and Bacchus. In a resort in Michigan, the Narcissus play is being presented, starring Niles Bradman, who only loves his career and himself. Brad Niles, his near-twin, loves him. Tom Apollo, a famous rock star, is here to rest his voice, and "Red" Bakis, who was formerly Tom's lover, is awaiting the arrival of Lord Rufus Harrington, the international impresario, who runs the resort. He is to back Tom or Red's new religious sect plans, each of which is opposite to the other. There is a youth, Danny Mead, who is loaned to the resort by Lord Rufus. He is killed by an arrow shot by Tom as he presents a display of his archery technique — Lord Rufus arrives. With the sacrifice — love — given by all participants, Danny is restored to life and gives happiness to all.

Two's Company by Steph Martin. Musical. Two acts. 2M.

The chronicle of seven years with two men whose relationship has "worked" — so far.

U

Underbelly Blues *(*formerly ***Night Fever****)* by Sebastian Stuart. Drama. One act. 6M, 1F. 1 exterior. $25/$10. Prod: Quaigh Theatre, New York, 1977.

The story of seven characters who come together one night on a deserted freeway on-ramp in South San Francisco. Glit and Stoney, the gay characters, are speed freaks determined to get to a party at any cost.

Union Dues by Paul J. Cyr. Drama. Three acts. 2M, 1F. 1 interior.

Joe lives in a house in Cambridge and is engaged to Helen, a nurse, and works for her father, who will give him his plumber's license in six months. She comes over to celebrate the six-month anniversary of their engagement and tells him of a letter her mother received from Peter, an old friend of Joe's. He invites him over, and after Helen goes to work, the two discuss their four-year relationship, which ended when Peter told Joe he loved him and asked him to move to New York with him. They make love and Joe plans to move to New York with Peter, admitting that he does love him. Helen discovers them, and Joe denies Peter; even though he loves Peter, he needs Helen and wants to marry her for appearance's sake, since he can't publicly admit he's gay.

V

Vieux Carré by Tennessee Williams. Drama. Full length. 4M, 5F. 1 interior. Prod: Playhouse Theatre, Nottingham, England, 1978. Publ: New Directions, New York, 1979. Agent: International Creative Management, Inc., 40 West 57th Street, New York, N.Y. 10019.

In the New Orleans French Quarter, the play focuses on various inhabitants of a dilapidated rooming house in the Vieux Carré: the comically desperate landlady, Mrs. Wire; Jane, a properly brought up young woman from New York making a last grab at pleasure with a vulgar but appealing strip-joint barker, Tye; two decayed gentlewomen politely starving in the garret; and the dying painter Nightingale, who tries to teach a young male writer something about love — both of the body and of the heart.

Visions of Kerouac by Martin Bauml Duberman. Drama-comedy. Two acts. 17M, 8F (Doubling). Abstract set. Negotiable. Prod: Lion Theatre Company, New York, 1976. Publ: Little, Brown and Company, Boston, 1977.

The story of the Beats, with the emphasis on their personal characters and relationships rather than their literary achievements. The central relationship of the play is that of Jack Kerouac and Neal Cassady. Through that relationship an attempt is made to suggest an archetypal pattern of male/male relationships in the United States: the deeply felt but emotionally blocked macho bond that destroys what it loves.

Visiting Hours by S. Michael Schnessel. Drama. Two acts. 5M, 2F. 1 interior. Negotiable. Prod: Omaha Community Playhouse, Omaha, Nebraska, 1979. Agent: Lucianne S. Goldberg, 255 West 84th Street, New York, N.Y. 10024.

Four men in their senior years are occupying a ward waiting for death: one is a ruthless businessman, now bitter because he blames his sons for the failure of his business; another is a homosexual who just lost his lover of 15 years and is grief-stricken over a legal battle in which his lover's will was invalidated; another is an alcholic trying to forget his cowardice at the 1924 Olympic Games; and the last is a Jew who lost everything to the Nazis. A six-year-old deaf-blind child wanders into the ward, and temporarily gives them new hope.

Walking Into the Dawn: A Celebration by Rochelle Holt Dubois. Comedy-drama. Full length. 5M, 5F. 1 interior. Prod: Magic Theatre, Omaha, Nebraska, 1975.

A consciousness play for after the women's revolution, it incorporates the idea that women have powerful standing inherited from the ancient goddesses.

War by Jean-Claude van Itallie. Drama. One act. 2M, 1F. 1 interior. $25. Prod: Barr-Albee-Wilder Playwright's Unit, New York, 1963. Publ and Agent: Dramatists Play Service.

Two actors, an older and a younger male, meet to improvise in the older actor's loft full of theatrical effects. The real or imagined visit of the lady down the hall is a maternal catalyst to their improvisations.

War Widow, The by Harvey Perr. Drama. One act. 1M (voice), 7F (Doubling). 4 interiors, 1 exterior. Prod: The Glines, New York, 1978. Agent: Flora Roberts, 65 East 55th Street, Suite 702, New York, N.Y. 10022.

A lonely and bored young woman, whose husband is abroad engaged in World War I, shares a stifling upper-class existence with her daughter and mother. On a trip to New York City, she meets a lesbian photographer and slowly, but quite surely, their friendship ripens into love and the young woman begins to find her own identity.

West of the Moon by Robert Heide. Drama. One act. 2M. 1 exterior. $35/$25. Prod: New Playwrights Theatre, New York, 1964.

Two men in a Christopher Street doorway in the rain, one a leather-jacket hustler drug-pusher/addict called Lucky, the other a Bible-belt schizoid innocent named Billy. The subtext is one of religious conversion in rural America meeting with street corruption in a big city.

West Street Gang, The by Doric Wilson. Comedy. Two acts. 14M, 2F (Doubling). 1 interior. $70/$50 (Negotiable). Prod: TOSOS Theatre Company, New York, 1977. Publ: in *Two Plays by Doric Wilson*, SeaHorse Press, New York, 1979. Agent: Terry Helbing, 51 West 4th Street, Room 300, New York, N.Y. 10012.

A polemical satire, focusing on the customers of a not-so-popular gay bar and their response and/or non-response to fag-bashing by neighborhood punks and other exploiters (gay and straight) including Anita Bryant.

What Is It, Zach? by James Purdy. Drama. One act. 2M. 1 interior. Prod: Herbert Berghof Studio Theatre, New York, 1979. Agent: Gilbert Parker, Curtis Brown Ltd., 575 Madison Avenue, New York, N.Y. 10022.

Set in an apartment in New York City, the play concerns a Vietnam veteran and a young man he took off the streets.

What's Wrong With You, Scuzzy? by Evan Senreich (book, music, and lyrics). Musical. Two acts. (Tape and lead sheets available.) 14M, 1F (Doubling). Unit set. Negotiable.

The story of a young man named Ian Varit. Through various scenes with his friends and relatives we are introduced to Ian, who is obsessed with his feelings of self-hate, suicide, and unexpressed homosexuality. He is tormented by memories of his youth. He finally manages to enter a gay bar and begins exploring the gay lifestyle, but then uses his homosexuality as new fuel for his self-hate. At the same time, he is rejected by his friends. Through a fantasy murder, Ian perceives that his own self-image has been his true enemy.

When Did You Last See My Mother? by Christopher Hampton. Drama. Full length. 3M, 2F. 1 interior. $50/$25. Prod: Comedy Theatre, London, 1966. Publ: Faber and Faber, London, 1967. Agent: Samuel French.

Jimmy is straight and his roommate, Ian, is gay, and the two bitch-fight constantly. Occasionally Jimmy's mother comes to visit. Jimmy and his girl ask Ian and another man to leave the apartment one night so they can make love; he refuses, Jimmy and Ian fight, and after a fight, they end their relationship. Jimmy's mother comes to see Ian, and before she can leave, a sexual attraction arises between them. She comes back later, asking Ian to make love to her, but leaves when she hears that her own son has homosexual proclivities. She rushes out in hysterics and kills herself in a car crash.

Who'll Carry the Banners When the Parade Passes By by Jasper Vance. Comedy-drama. Two acts. 9M, 2F. 1 interior.

At an anniversary party for a gay male couple who've been together for year, another, more conservative gay couple decides to attend, trying to get back into the current social scene. They discover that they don't fit into a setting they don't understand.

Widows and Children First by Harvey Fierstein. Comedy. Two acts. 3M, 1F. 1 interior. $50/$35. Prod: La Mama E.T.C., New York, 1979. Agent: Helen Merrill, 337 West 22nd Street, New York, N.Y. 10011.

The conclusion of the "Torch Song Trilogy." Set five years after **Fugue In a Nursery** (q.v.), this play focuses on the social and romantic themes of the other two plays in the trilogy, and on Arnold and his relationships with his adopted fifteen-year-old gay son, his mother and his ex-lover.

Willa-Willie-Bill's Dope Garden by Megan Terry. Drama. One act. 4F. 1 exterior. Prod: Griffith Park, Los Angeles, 1975. Publ: in *Christopher Street,* New York, June 1978.

A meditation in one act on Willa Cather in which four lesbians travel through the woods to find the spot where, in 1938, Willa Cather used to write. When they find it, they share grass and wine and make love in her honor.

Window, The by Frank Marcus. Drama. One act. 3M. 1 interior. $10. Prod: Ambiance Theatre, London, 1970. Publ and Agent: Samuel French.

Every night a neighbor comes to the apartment of a blind recluse to report what he sees through binoculars happening in the apartment of the girl who rejected the recluse. And every night the neighbor reports a different man calling on the girl: she has obviously turned to prostitution, and the recluse is infuriated. But one night, a second visitor, female, appears through the binoculars, and for the first time the blinds are lowered. However, the neighbor voyeur is really homosexual and the girl in the apartment is non-existent; this is his way at getting back at heterosexuals, by detailing the infidelities of women.

"... With Female Impersonator Bublz La Rue As Star ..." by Ross H. Jones. Drama. Two acts. 10M, 1F (Doubling). 1 interior. Negotiable.

After Bublz La Rue finishes the last of her evening performances, she returns to the dressing room to remove costume and make-up, while recounting the story of his/her life, involving his mother, father, brother, lover, First Commanding Officer, et al. Bublz/Jimmy leaves home, comes out and is thrown out of his house by his father. As he gets out of drag and into his male drag, he remembers his father's death and the beginning of his life as a professional entertainer.

Wives, The by Richard James Henry. Drama. One act. 2M. 2 exteriors. $30/$20.

In a futuristic society, two men are lovers in a world that forbids homosexuality and orders that all men must marry by their twenty-fifth birthday or be sent into slavery. One of the men has visited a more liberal planet and has found a solution to their dilemma: life-like female robots who will be the men's "wives" and act as cover for their relationship.

Wonderful Happy Days by James Purdy. Drama. One act. 2M, 1F. 1 interior. Prod: Herbert Berghof Studio Theatre, New York, 1979. Publ: in *Out of a Clear Blue Sky,* New London Press, Dallas, Texas, 1980. Agent: Gilbert Parker, Curtis Brown Ltd., 575 Madison Avenue, New York, N.Y. 10022.

The play concerns the anguish caused by the younger of two brothers who has committed a crime in order to save the home they live in with their mother.

Wonderful Lives! by James B. Ferguson (book, music and lyrics). Musical. Two acts. (Sheet music available.) 7M, 7F. 4 interiors, 7 exteriors. Negotiable. Prod: The Glines, New York, 1977.

Adele and Richard are best friends and roommates. She's straight, he's gay. She's a famous archeologist and magazine publisher; he's a famous mystery writer. The play is about their special relationship and about how, by taking risks and refusing to compromise, they get what they want out of life. Both of them meet men and fall in love, and settle in with their new partners, but miss living together. Each relationship runs into serious problems, but at the end, a solution has been reached: Adele and Richard are roommates again, but each still has their romantic partner.

World Is My Body, The by Harry H. Long and Joseph Uher. Documentary. Full length. 2M. Minimal set.

Subtitled "readings from gay history and literature," the piece is a tribute to lesbian and gay writers of all periods that explore the many moods and colors of being gay, of interest to all gay women and men.

Xircus!: The Private Life of Jesus Christ by Donald Brooks. Drama. One act. 11M, 4F (Doubling). Various interiors, exteriors. Prod: St. Peter's Church, New York, 1971.

X, the hero of the play who represents Christ, is brought back to earth as a young man in Times Square, who has a variety of straight and gay experiences in a series of mixed-media episodes. Each episode has a parallel story in the Bible.

Y

Your Town by Daniel Curzon. Satire. One act. 3M, 2F. Minimal set. Negotiable. Prod: Earnest Players, San Francisco, 1978.

A satirical look at typical family life (Mom, Dad, Sis, Junior) by a Narrator who traces the courting, mating, child-rearing, death, and repetition of the cycle by the children. The offspring are represented by stuffed frogs that are thrown on the stage throughout the action, ending with a deluge of frogs.

APPENDIX A
"Lost" Plays

The following is an alphabetical listing by title of plays for which complete information could not be obtained, and therefore could not be included in the main listings. Either the playwright could not be located to be sent a form, or a form was sent and the playwright did not respond.

Alive and Well in Argentina by Barry Pritchard
And Puppy Dog Tails by David Gaard
Bayou by Medusa's Revenge
Bill and William by James Addison
Bitches, The by Eduardo Corbé
Bluebird by Ted Menten
Boy Named Dog, A by Joseph Renard
Brothers and Sisters by James Ackerson, music by Darryl Curry
Circle in the Water by Gerry Raad
Cocteau by Andy Milligan
Compulsion by Meyer Levin
Cup of Tea by Raymond P. Comeau
Dear Oscar by Caryl G. Young and Addy O. Fieger
Dime Store Diamonds by Jeff Hochhauser
Disturbance of Mirrors, A by P. S. Staten
Divorce of Judy and Jane, The by Arthur Whitney
Eustace Chisholm and the Works, adapted by Adrian Hall from the novel by James Purdy
Evil That Men Do by Ed Jacobs
Foreplay by Robert M. Lane
Funny Walk Home, A by Jeff Weiss
Geese by Gus Weill
Going Slow by Medusa's Revenge
Grab Bag, The by Robert J. Thompson
Home Away From, A by Glenn Allen Smith
How Are Things With the Walking Wounded? by Tom Hendry
International Wrestling Match by Jeff Weiss
King of the Mountain by Raymond P. Comeau
Land Where Our Fathers Died by J. J. Coyle
Last Chance at the Brass Ring by Sidney Morris
Lightning Bug Convention, The by Morgan Tyler
Mirror Mirror by Diana Frolov
My Name Is Oscar Wilde by Norman Holland
Over the Hill by Lonnie Burr

116 GAY THEATRE ALLIANCE

Penda's Fen by David Rudkin
Porn Play by Elmer Kline
Pushover: An Old-Fashioned Homosexual Mystery by Jeff Weiss
Quaint Honour by Robert Gelbert
Queer Things by Ed Kuczewski
Season in Hell, A by Robert Payne
Section Nine by Philip Magdalany
So Who's Goldberg? by Louis del Grande
Special Delivery by Donald Driver
Special Gifts by Robin Jones
Spiro Who? by William Meyers
Strawberry Fields by Mike Hollingsworth
That's How the Rent Gets Paid by Jeff Weiss
Touch of God in the Golden Age by John Palmer
Under the Cross-Eyed Eagle by Elmer Kline
War Games by Neal Weaver
Will, The by Elmer Kline
Winter Foliage by David Michaels

APPENDIX B

Gay Theatre Companies

As of December, 1979, the following is a list of active lesbian or gay theatre companies:

Apollo's Mice
P.O. Box 29422
Los Angeles, CA 90029

Cambridge Lesbian Theatre
217 Elm Street
Cambridge, MA 02139

Earnest Players
c/o Turner
3851 21st Street
San Francisco, CA 94114

Folsom Street Warehouse Theatre
280 Seventh Street
San Francisco, CA 94103

Gay Sweatshop Theatre Company
34 South Molton Street
London, W1, England

The Gay Theatre
c/o Scott
P.O. Box 22
Kings Cross 2010
New South Wales, Australia

The Glines
28 Willow Street
Brooklyn, N.Y. 11201

Lambda Productions
P.O. Box 18728
Denver, CO 80218

Medusa's Revenge
10 Bleecker Street
New York, N.Y. 10012

118 GAY THEATRE ALLIANCE

Montrose Players
Montrose Activity Center
1423 Holman
Houston, TX 77004

Out and About Theatre Company
2301 East Franklin
Minneapolis, MN 55406

Playhouse on the Mall
390 Pomona Mall East
Pomona, CA 91766

Theatre Rhinoceros
Goodman Building
1115 Geary Street
San Francisco, CA 94109

The following are not gay theatre companies, but regularly do gay plays:

Back Alley Theatre
1365 Kennedy Street, N.W.
Washington, D.C. 20011

The Fourth "E" Company
c/o Young
400 West 43rd Street, #27H
New York, N.Y. 10036

Ted Williams
19 Hartpury Avenue
Elwood, Melbourne
Australia 3184

INDEX OF PLAYWRIGHTS

Ackerson, James, App. A
Addison, James, App. A
Addyman, Elizabeth, 45
Albee, Edward, 13, 62
Allen, Seth, 90
Allyn, Eric, 80
Andersen, Dennis R., 63
Anderson, Robert, 97
Arnold, C. D., 33, 85
Arnold, John, 32, 79, 81

Babe, Thomas, 81
Bagnold, Enid, 19, 64
Baker, Roger, 54, 66
Banacki, Raymond, 70
Baraka, Imamu Amiri, 13, 99
Barton, Lee, 70
Bateman, Lane, 57, 61
Behan, Brendan, 50
Bentley, Eric, 60
Birimisa, George, 28, 31, 33, 43, 65, 80, 84
Bobrick, Sam, 71
Bollow, Ludmilla, 63
Bourdet, Edouard, 20
Bowen, John, 101
Brecht, Bertolt, 34, 56
Brooks, Donald, 112
Brown, Arch, 69
Bumbalo, Victor, 57
Buono, Carmine J., 31, 40
Burr, Lonnie, App. A

Caine, Christopher, 50
Camicia, J., 74
Carideo, Ralph, 58, 67, 93, 100
Carmines, Al, 37
Carter, Randolph, 52, 87, 92

Cernos, Bob, 43
Chambers, Jane, 58
Chancey, Susie, 39
Chayefsky, Paddy, 58
Clark, Ron, 71
Collinson, Laurence, 98
Colmar, Andrew, 29
Combs, Frederick, 22
Comeau, Raymond P., App. A
Corbé, Eduardo, App. A
Coward, Noel, 32, 92
Coyle, J. J., App. A
Crew, Louie, 66
Cristofer, Michael, 89
Crowley, Mart, 16
Crutchley, Kate, 9
Csontos, David, 25, 73, 90
Curry, Darryl, App. A
Curzon, Daniel, 14, 25, 31, 88, 112
Cyr, Paul J., 104

Dailey, Jeff, 14
Davies, June Wyndham, 45
deHelen, Sandra, 14
Delaney, Shelagh, 97
Delgado, Ramon, 55, 73
delValle, Peter, 61
de Lyons, Eric, 75
Dentinger, Jr., John A., 102
Diaman, N. A., 11
Driver, Donald, App. A
Duberman, Martin Bauml, 24, 34, 35, 46, 65, 77, 84, 105
Dubois, Rochelle Holt, 44, 60, 107
Duncan, Ronald, 21

Dunster, Mark, 23, 33, 66, 69, 85
Dyer, Charles, 93

Ensana, Joel, 21, 59, 101
Eppendorfer, Hans, 59
Erickson, Richard, 17, 94
Esposito, Robert, 55, 100
Eulo, Ken, 38

Feiffer, Jules, 60
Fenkel, R., 32
Ferguson, James B., 111
Fieger, Addy O., App. A
Fierstein, Harvey, 20, 39, 41, 54, 109
Fish, C. C., 89
Fornes, Maria Irene, 38
Foster, Paul, 87
Fox, Martin, 72
Frauman, Barry, 94
Friedman, Bruce Jay, 93
Frolov, Diana, App. A
Fugate, James (Barr), 42
Fuller, Henry, B., 12

Gaard, David, App. A
Gass, Ken, 16
Gath, Joseph, 61, 80
Gay Men's Theatre Collective, 27
Gelbert, Robert, App. A
Gibbs, Wolcott, 88
Glaister, Larry, 60
Glines, John, 46
Goetz, Ruth and Augustus, 52
Goldberg, Dick, 37
Goldsmith, Lee, 89
Gottesfeld, Laury Ann, 70
Gray, Richard, 54, 67
Gray, Simon, 18
Greco, Steven, 46
Greig, Noel, 12, 30, 74
Griffiths, Drew, 9, 12, 30, 54, 56, 66, 74
Griggs, Barry, 48

Hagen, Reigh, 65
Hakim, Eleanor, 59
Hall, Adrian, App. A
Hall, Richard, 60, 69, 78, 81
Hamilton, Wallace, 47, 54, 66, 83
Hampton, Christopher, 100, 109
Harrington, Y., 96
Harris, J. Neil, 101
Harris, Kenneth, 22, 103
Heide, Robert, 10, 14, 53, 108
Hellman, Lillian, 22
Henry, Richard James, 72, 110
Herbert, John, 24, 40, 78
Hill, Kathy Burke, 90
Hobbs, J. Kline, 73
Hochhauser, Jeff, App. A
Hoffman, William M., 26, 43, 44
Hogan, Frank, 91
Holland, Anthony, 26
Holland, Frank, 15
Holland, Norman, App. A
Hopkins, John, 38
Hunter, Paul, 47

Innaurato, Albert, 42

Jackson, Graham, 63, 98
Jacobs, Ed, App. A
Janz, Milli, 36
Jones, LeRoi, 13, 99
Jones, Robin, 46, App. A
Jones, Ross H., 93, 99, 110

Kammer, Kerry, 28
Kardish, Larry, 18
Kasten, Kate, 14, 73
Katz, Jonathan, 25
Katz, Philip, 29
Kazmayer, Robert Lynn, 48, 79, 88
Kilroy, Thomas, 31
King, Philip, 50
Kingsley, Stuart, 35
Kirkwood, James, 82
Kline, Elmer, App. A

DIRECTORY OF GAY PLAYS 121

Kronengold, A. J., 51, 102
Kubran, Walter, 91
Kuczewski, Ed, App. A

Lane, Robert M., App. A
Laurence, Charles, 67
Laurents, Arthur, 35
Lee, Jim, 64
Lee, Leslie, 39
Lee, Lonnie W., 77, 99
Levin, Meyer, App. A
Levine, Ross, M., 20
Lim, Paul Stephen, 22, 25, 49, 80
Lind, Jakov, 36
Lishans, Arie, 29
Long, Harry H., 10, 37, 94, 111
Lotman, Loretta, 78, 98, 100
Ludlam, Charles, 20

MacLean, Ross, 36, 40, 69, 91
Magdalany, Philip, App. A
Magowan, Stephen, 10
Marasco, Robert, 23
Marcus, Frank, 57, 110
Marley, Mentha III, 18
Marlowe, Christopher, 34
Martin, Steph, 10, 24, 41, 103
McCullers, Carson, 13
McHenry, Mark, 48, 94
McIlnay, Dean, 17, 94
McNally, Terrence, 71, 86
Medusa's Revenge, App. A
Melrose, Ronald, 40
Menten, Ted, App. A
Meyers, William, App. A
Michaels, David, App. A
Miller, Susan, 25, 68
Milligan, Andy, App. A
Mitchell, David, 29
Morris, Sidney, App. A
Morrison, Coleman, 44
Muchmore, Wes, 90
Myers, Steven J., 15, 27, 53

Orton, Joe, 35, 86
Osborne, John, 77
Ost, Bob, 17

Palmer, John, App. A
Patricca, Nicholas, A., 36
Patrick, Robert, 11, 32, 39, 41, 48, 51, 56, 61, 65, 73, 102
Payne, Robert, App. A
Pearlstein, Dennis, 69
Perr, Harvey, 43, 89, 108
Pescatore, Angela, 44
Peterson, Gregory, 83
Pink Satin Bombers, 79
Pinter, Harold, 24
Posener, Jill, 11
Pritchard, Barry, App. A
Puchall, Larry, 65
Pugliese, Carol, 75
Puliafito, Fred, 76
Purdy, James, 9, 15, 23, 29, 50, 62, 88, 101, 108, 111, App. A

Raad, Gerry, App. A
Rabe, David, 95
Real, Philip, 17, 84
Renard, Joseph, App. A
Robertson, Lanie, 27
Rochester John Wilmot, Earl of, 91
Ronan, Richard, 19, 22, 23, 49
Roome, Douglas Derek, 66, 90
Rosenthal, Andrew, 99
Rossett, Alan, 102
Rudkin, David, App. A
Russell, Bill, 40

Sawyer, Michael, 15, 68
Schnessel, S. Michael, 30, 106
Scoppetone, Sandra, 49
Scott, Arthur, 76
Senreich, Evan, 109
Shairp, Mordaunt, 45
Sherman, Martin, 14, 77

122   GAY THEATRE ALLIANCE

Shivers, Rob, 30
Silver, Fred, 53
Sisley, Emily L., 41
Smith, David Emerson, 85
Smith, Glenn Allen, App. A
Smith, Michael, 26
Solly, Bill, 16
Spencer, Colin, 92
Staab, Jane, 31
Staten, P. S., App. A
Stephan, Fredric, 81
Sterner, Steve, 61
Steward, Barry, 95
Stringer, Alan, 11
Stuart, Sebastian, 67, 104

Tavel, Ronald, 75
Taylor, Richard, 48
Terry, Megan, 26, 110
Thompson, Robert J., App. A
Tremblay, Michel, 49
Turner, Daniel, 25
Tyler, Morgan, App. A

Uher, Joseph, 10, 37, 94, 111

Vanase, Paul, 33
Vance, Jasper, 109
vanItallie, Jean-Claude, 107

Wakeman, Alan, 89
Wallace, Robert, 44, 70, 91
Wandor, Micheline, 20
Ward, Donald, 16
Weaver, Neal, App. A
Weill, Gus, App. A
Weiss, Jeff, App. A
West, Mae, 33
Whitmore, George, 21, 59, 86
Whitney, Arthur, App. A
Wilcox, Michael, 85
Williams, Gerald Ray, 64
Williams, Tennessee, 2, 105
Williams, William Carlos, 63

Wilmot, John, Earl of
    Rochester, 91
Wilson, Doric, 9, 40, 71, 78,
    95, 108
Wilson, Lanford, 1, 45, 62
Wilson, Owen, 10
Wilson, R. Dale, 98
Wolverton, Terry, et al., 74

Yeomans, Cal, 26, 53, 74, 81,
    86, 92, 95
Young, Caryl G., App. A

Zaikis, Shelly, 79

GAY THEATRE ALLIANCE

Northeast Region

51 West 4th Street, Room 300
New York, New York 10012

(212) 598-2597

DIRECTORY OF GAY PLAYS

Listing Form

TITLE OF PLAY_____

PLAYWRIGHT_____

TYPE (Drama, comedy, musical, etc.)_____ACTS (#)_____

If musical, is score available for review?_____

If so, in what form? (Tape, sheet music, etc.)_____

CHARACTERS: Male (#) _____ Female (#)_____ Doubling possible?_____

SETTINGS: Interiors (#) _____ Exteriors (#) _____

ROYALTIES: First performance $_____ Subsequent performances $_____

NAME AND ADDRESS OF AGENT (If none, write "author"):_____

_____

IF PRODUCED, PRODUCING COMPANY, LOCATION AND DATE OF FIRST PRODUCTION:

_____

_____

IF PUBLISHED, TITLE OF VOLUME, PUBLISHER AND DATE OF PUBLICATION:

_____

_____

PLOT SYNOPSIS: (Continue on reverse; synopsis may be edited to fit space requirements.)

GAY THEATRE ALLIANCE

Northeast Region

51 West 4th Street, Room 300
New York, New York 10012

(212) 598-2597

DIRECTORY OF GAY PLAYS

Listing Form

TITLE OF PLAY _____

PLAYWRIGHT _____

TYPE (Drama, comedy, musical, etc.)_____ ACTS (#)_____

If musical, is score available for review?_____

If so, in what form? (Tape, sheet music, etc.)_____

CHARACTERS: Male (#) _____ Female (#)_____ Doubling possible?_____

SETTINGS: Interiors (#) _____ Exteriors (#) _____

ROYALTIES: First performance $_____ Subsequent performances $_____

NAME AND ADDRESS OF AGENT (If none, write "author"):_____

_____

IF PRODUCED, PRODUCING COMPANY, LOCATION AND DATE OF FIRST PRODUCTION:

_____

_____

IF PUBLISHED, TITLE OF VOLUME, PUBLISHER AND DATE OF PUBLICATION:

_____

_____

PLOT SYNOPSIS: (Continue on reverse; synopsis may be edited to fit space requirements.)

GAY THEATRE ALLIANCE

Northeast Region

51 West 4th Street, Room 300
New York, New York 10012

(212) 598-2597

DIRECTORY OF GAY PLAYS

Listing Form

TITLE OF PLAY _____

PLAYWRIGHT _____

TYPE (Drama, comedy, musical, etc.) _____ ACTS (#) _____

If musical, is score available for review? _____

If so, in what form? (Tape, sheet music, etc.) _____

CHARACTERS: Male (#) _____ Female (#) _____ Doubling possible? _____

SETTINGS: Interiors (#) _____ Exteriors (#) _____

ROYALTIES: First performance $ _____ Subsequent performances $ _____

NAME AND ADDRESS OF AGENT (If none, write "author"): _____
_____

IF PRODUCED, PRODUCING COMPANY, LOCATION AND DATE OF FIRST PRODUCTION:
_____
_____

IF PUBLISHED, TITLE OF VOLUME, PUBLISHER AND DATE OF PUBLICATION:
_____
_____

PLOT SYNOPSIS: (Continue on reverse; synopsis may be edited to fit space requirements.)

Coming from

JH PRESS

The *Gay Theatre Alliance Directory of Gay Plays* is the first publication of JH Press, a new gay publishing company specializing in gay theatre publications.

In the coming months, JH Press will be publishing a series of play scripts of significant gay theatre productions by major gay playwrights. These scripts will be published as single-play acting editions, to be used for production purposes by theatre companies; they will also be available to the general public in gay and theatre bookstores.

JH Press will also handle the amateur leasing rights to these plays, making it the first company to fulfill this function exclusively for gay plays.

JH Press is also a member of the Gay Presses of New York, a new cooperative effort to promote gay publishing. JH Press joins with Calamus Books (publisher of *The Faggots and Their Friends Between Revolutions* by Larry Mitchell, *Mercy Drop and Other Plays* by Robert Patrick, and other books), and SeaHorse Press (publisher of *The Deformity Lover and Other Poems* by Felice Picano and *Two Plays by Doric Wilson*, and other books) in an attempt to increase visibility of the gay press through mutual advertising, promotion, sales and distribution.

About the Type

Gay Theatre Alliance Directory of Gay Plays was set in Megaron medium, bold italic and extra bold on the AM Varityper Comp/Set 4510-W direct-entry phototypesetting system. Composition by Verl Dunn and Chuck Partridge: Foto-Ready Production, a full-service — design & illustration/editorial/composition/manufacturing — studio.

Printed and bound by Faculty Press, Brooklyn, New York.